Collins

Work on your
Vocabulary
Upper Intermediate B2

Collins

HarperCollins Publishers
The News Building
1 London Bridge Street
London SE1 9GF

First edition 2013

10 9 8 7 6 5 4 3 2

© HarperCollins Publishers 2013

ISBN 978-0-00-749965-6

Collins® is a registered trademark of HarperCollins Publishers Limited

www.collinselt.com

A catalogue record for this book is available from the British Library

Typeset in India by Aptara

Printed and bound by CPI Group (UK) Ltd, Croydon

All rights reserved. No part of this book may be reproduced, stored in a retrieval system, or transmitted in any form or by any means, electronic, mechanical, photocopying, recording or otherwise, without the prior permission in writing of the Publisher. This book is sold subject to the conditions that it shall not, by way of trade or otherwise, be lent, re-sold, hired out or otherwise circulated without the Publisher's prior consent in any form of binding or cover other than that in which it is published and without a similar condition including this condition being imposed on the subsequent purchaser.

HarperCollins does not warrant that www.collinselt.com or any other website mentioned in this title will be provided uninterrupted, that any website will be error free, that defects will be corrected, or that the website or the server that makes it available are free of viruses or bugs. For full terms and conditions please refer to the site terms provided on the website.

Language Testing 123
Specialists in Assessment and e-Learning

The material in this book has been written by a team from Language Testing 123, a UK-based consultancy that specializes in English language assessment and materials. The units are by Elizabeth Walter and have been based on material from the Collins Corpus and the Collins COBUILD reference range.

www.languagetesting123.co

Contents

Introduction		5
	Is this the right book for me?	5
	What does this book contain?	5
	I'm a student: how can I use this book?	5
	Study tips	6
	I want to improve my vocabulary	6
	I'm a teacher: how can I use this book with my classes?	7
	Lesson plan	7
	Guide to word classes	9
1	British and American English words and phrases	10
2	Entertainment and the media	14
3	Places and buildings	17
4	Relationships	21
5	Beliefs and ideas	24
6	Social and political issues	27
7	Experiences	31
8	News and current affairs	35
9	The natural world	39
10	Natural phenomena	42
11	House and home	45
12	Health, medicine and exercise	49
13	Feelings	52
14	Music and the arts	55
15	Crime and law	59
16	Communication	63
17	Words and phrases for linking ideas	66
18	Work and jobs	70
19	Travel and holidays	73
20	Prefixes and suffixes	77
21	Register – formal vs. informal	81
22	Words that are used together (collocations)	84
23	Education	87
24	Information technology	91
25	Services	94
26	People	97
27	Seeing, hearing, touching, smelling and tasting	100

28	Movement and speed	103
29	Phrases with *be*, *do*, *get*, *have* and *make*	106
30	Metaphorical language	110

Answer key	114
Pronunciation guide	121
Index	122

Introduction

Welcome to *Work on your Vocabulary – Upper Intermediate (B2)*.

Is this the right book for me?

This book, *Work on your Vocabulary – Upper Intermediate (B2)*, helps students to learn and practise English vocabulary at CEF level B2. This book is suitable for you to use if you are at CEF level B2, or just below.

So, what is CEF level B2? Well, there are six Common European Framework levels. They go up from A1 for beginners, A2, B1, B2, C1 and finally C2.

If the description below sounds like you, then this is probably the right book for you. If not, choose *Work on your Vocabulary – Intermediate (B1)* (below this level) or *Work on your Vocabulary – Advanced (C1)* (above this level).

- I can understand most of the words and expressions when I read texts on many subjects, especially when they are about my areas of knowledge and interest.
- I can have conversations with native speakers of English and other good speakers in a quite natural way.
- I'm aware that I make mistakes, but other people usually understand what I want to say or write.
- I think I know quite a lot of vocabulary, but I also believe that there is a lot more to learn.

What does this book contain?

This book contains 30 units to help you learn and practise important vocabulary for this upper intermediate (B2) level.

Each unit gives you **explanations** and **definitions** of the words and expressions for the topic area, in the **Word Finder** boxes

There is a series of **exercises** that give you useful practice in this particular area.

The **answers** to all the exercises are at the back of the book.

At the back of the book, you'll also find a list of all the words introduced in the book (the **index**). Each word has the unit number next to it, so you can find it easily in the main part of the book.

The index also includes phonetics, to help you pronounce the words correctly. There is also a **pronunciation guide** to help you read and understand the phonetic symbols.

There are **Good to know!** boxes to help you to pay attention to important information about the words and expressions.

I'm a student: how can I use this book?

You can use this book in different ways. It depends on your needs, and the time that you have.

- If you have a teacher, he or she may give you some advice about using the book.

- If you are working alone, you may decide to study the complete book from beginning to end, starting with unit 1 and working your way through to the end.
- You might find that it is better to choose which units you need to study first, which might not be the first units in the book. Take control of what you learn and choose the units you feel are most important for you.
- You may also decide to use the book for reference when you are not sure about a particular vocabulary topic.
- You can find what you want to learn about by looking in the **Contents** page.
- Please note that, if you do not understand something in one unit, you may need to study a unit earlier in the book for more explanation.

Study tips

1 Read the aim and introduction to the unit carefully.
2 Read the explanation. Sometimes, there is a short text or dialogue; sometimes there are tables of information; sometimes there are examples with notes. These are to help you understand the most important information about this area of vocabulary.
3 Don't read the explanation too quickly: spend time trying to understand it as well as you can. If you don't understand, read it again more slowly.
4 Do the exercises. Don't do them too quickly: think carefully about the answers. If you don't feel sure, look at the explanation and Word Finder box again. Write your answers in pencil, or, even better, on a separate piece of paper. (This means that you can do the exercises again later.)
5 Check your answers to the exercises in the back of the book.
6 If you get every answer correct, congratulations! Don't worry if you make some mistakes. Studying your mistakes is an important part of learning.
7 Look carefully at each mistake: can you now see why the correct answer is what it is?
8 Read the explanation and definitions again to help you understand.
9 Finally, if the unit includes a **Good to Know!** box, then try really hard to remember what it says. It contains a special piece of information about the words and expressions.
10 Always return: come back and do the unit's exercises again a few days later. This helps you to keep the information in your head for longer.

I want to improve my vocabulary

Good! Only using one book won't be enough to really make your vocabulary improve. The most important thing is you!

Buy a good dictionary for your level. You could try the *Collins COBUILD Advanced Dictionary of English*.

Of course, you need to have a notebook, paper or electronic. Try these six techniques for getting the best from it.

- *Make it personal*: When you're learning a new word or expression, try to write some examples about yourself or people or places you know. It's easier to remember sentences about your life than someone else's! For example, *I have one older brother and two younger sisters*.

Introduction

- *Look out*: Everything you read or hear in English may contain some examples of the new vocabulary you're learning. Try to notice these examples. Also, try to write down some of these examples, so that you can learn them.
- *Think aloud*: Practise saying the new words aloud. It helps you to remember them better. Also, pronunciation is very important; people need to understand you!
- *Everywhere you go*: Take your notebook with you. Use spare moments, such as when you're waiting for a friend to arrive. Read through your notes. Try to repeat things from memory. A few minutes here and there adds up to a useful learning system.
- *Take it further*: Don't just learn the examples in the book. Keep making your own examples, and learning those.
- *Don't stop*: It's really important to keep learning. If you don't keep practising, you won't remember for very long. Practise the new vocabulary today, tomorrow, the next day, a week later and a month later.

I'm a teacher: how can I use this book with my classes?

The contents have been very carefully selected by experts from Language Testing 123, using the Common European Framework for Reference, English Profile, the British Council Core Inventory, the Collins Corpus and the Collins COBUILD dictionaries range. As such, it represents a useful body of knowledge for students to acquire at this level. The language used is designed to be of effective general relevance and interest to any learner aged 14+.

The exercises use a range of types to engage with students and to usefully practise what they have learnt from the explanation pages on the left. There are enough exercises for each unit that it is not necessary for students to do all the exercises at one sitting. Rather, you may wish to return in later sessions to complete the remaining exercises.

The book will be a valuable self-study resource for students studying on their own. You can also integrate it into the teaching that you provide for your students.

The explanations and exercises, while designed for self-study, can be easily adapted by you to provide useful interactive work for your students in class.

You will probably use the units in the book to extend, back up or consolidate language work you are doing in class. This means you will probably make a careful choice about which unit to do at a particular time.

You may also find that you recommend certain units to students who are experiencing particular difficulty with specific language areas. Alternatively, you may use various units in the book as an aid to revision.

Lesson plan

1 Read the aim and introduction to the unit carefully: is it what you want your students to focus on? Make sure the students understand it.
2 Go through the explanation with your students. You may read this aloud to them, or ask them to read it silently to themselves. With a confident class, you could ask them to read some of it aloud.

3. If there is a dialogue, you could ask students to perform it. If there is a text, you could extend it in some way that makes it particularly relevant to your students. Certainly, you should provide a pronunciation model of focus language.

4. Take time over the explanation page, and check students' understanding. Use concept-checking questions.

5. Perhaps do the first exercise together with the class. Don't do it too quickly: encourage students to think carefully about the answers. If they don't feel sure, look together at the explanation again.

6. Now get students to do the other exercises. They can work alone, or perhaps in pairs, discussing the answers. This will involve useful speaking practice and also more careful consideration of the information. Tell students to write their answers in pencil, or, even better, on a separate piece of paper. (This means that they can do the exercises again later.)

7. Check their answers to the exercises in the back of the book. Discuss the questions and problems they have.

8. If the unit includes a **Good to know!** box, then tell students to try really hard to remember what it says. It contains a special piece of information about the words and expressions.

9. Depending on your class and the time available, there are different ways you could extend the learning. If one of the exercises is in the form of an email, you could ask your students to write a reply to it. If the exercises are using spoken language, then you can ask students to practise these as bits of conversation. They can re-write the exercises with sentences that are about themselves and each other. Maybe pairs of students can write an exercise of their own together and these can be distributed around the class. Maybe they can write little stories or dialogues including the focus language and perform these to the class.

10. Discuss with the class what notes they should make about the language in the unit. Encourage them to make effective notes, perhaps demonstrating this on the board for them, and/or sharing different ideas from the class.

11. Always return: come back and repeat at least some of the unit's exercises again a few days later. This helps your students to keep the information in their heads for longer.

Guide to word classes

All the words in **Word Finder** boxes have a word class. The table below gives you more information about each of these word classes.

Word class	Description
ADJECTIVE	An adjective is a word that is used for telling you more about a person or thing. You use adjectives to talk about appearance, colour, size, or other qualities, e.g. *He has got **short** hair.*
ADVERB	An adverb is a word that gives more information about when, how, or where something happens, e.g. *She went **inside**.*
NOUN	A noun is a word that refers to a person, a thing, or a quality, e.g. *I live in the **city**.*
PHRASAL VERB	A phrasal verb consists of a verb and one or more particles, e.g. *When I go outside, I **put on** a warm coat.*
PHRASE	Phrases are groups of words which are used together and which have a meaning of their own, e.g. *I **would like** to get a new job.*
VERB	A verb is a word that is used for saying what someone or something does, or what happens to them, or to give information about them, e.g. *Can I **pay** by credit card?*

British and American English words and phrases

Although British and American people all speak English, there are many differences in the words they use, the way they use them and the way they spell them.

This letter is written by an American woman.

> Boston, September 2013
>
> Dear Alice
>
> I hope you're looking forward to your **vacation** with us here in Boston. I'm sure you will love it. It's so beautiful here in the **fall**, with all the leaves turning red and gold!
>
> You'll be amazed when you see how much Bradley has grown – he only has two more **semesters** in high school. I can't wait to see your kids again! Tell them that they'll have plenty to do when they're here. There's a **movie theater** in the next block, and our **apartment** is close to the **downtown** area of the city. They'll be able to get around easily on the **subway**.
>
> Lots of love
> Carol

This email is written by a British man.

From: Peter Kennedy
To: Darren Cox
Subject: Nearly home!

Hi Darren

Just a quick email to say that Gemma and I will be back from our travels on November 13th. I can't say we're looking forward to returning to a damp, British **autumn**! I know I can't complain when we've been away for six months – we've had the most fantastic **holiday**, as you can imagine.

The best bits for me were the **railway** journeys in India – the scenery and the whole experience were fantastic. Russia was really interesting – you should see the Moscow **underground** – the stations are amazing!

We're looking forward to seeing you and all our other friends soon, though it was great being able to keep in touch by email – when I travelled as a student, I remember having to arrange to pick up **post** from my parents in various strange places!

Anyway, if you could just call in at the **flat** and put the heating on a few days before we get back, that would be great.

See you then
Pete

UNIT 1 British and American English words and phrases

British and American English words and phrases

	autumn (UK) / fall (US)	NOUN **Autumn** is the season between summer and winter when the weather becomes cooler and the leaves fall off the trees.
	bill (UK) / check (US)	NOUN A **bill** is a written statement of money that you owe for goods or services.
	biscuit (UK) / cookie (US)	NOUN A **biscuit** is a small flat cake that is crisp and usually sweet.
	chips (UK) / fries, French fries (US)	NOUN **Chips** are long, thin pieces of potato that are fried and eaten hot.
	cinema (UK) / movie theater (US)	NOUN A **cinema** is a place where people go to watch films for entertainment.
	city centre, town centre (UK) / downtown (US)	NOUN The **city centre** is the busiest part of a city, where most of the shops and businesses are.
	crisps (UK) / potato chips (US)	NOUN **Crisps** are very thin slices of potato that are fried and eaten cold.
	film (UK) / movie (UK & US)	NOUN A **film** consists of moving pictures that have been recorded so that they can be shown at the cinema or on television.
	flat (UK) / apartment (UK & US)	NOUN A **flat** is a set of rooms for living in, usually on one floor and part of a larger building.
	ground floor (UK) / first floor (US)	NOUN The **ground floor** is the floor of a building that is at the same level as the ground outside.
	holiday (UK) / vacation (US)	NOUN A **holiday** is a period of time during which you relax and enjoy yourself away from home.
	interval (UK) / intermission (US)	NOUN An **interval** during a film, concert, show, or game is a short break between two of the parts.
	lift (UK) / elevator (US)	NOUN A **lift** is a device that carries people or goods up and down inside tall buildings.
	mobile, mobile phone (UK) / cellphone (US)	NOUN A **mobile phone** is a telephone that you carry with you.
	pavement (UK) / sidewalk (US)	NOUN A **pavement** is a path with a hard surface, usually by the side of a road.
	post (UK) / mail (US)	NOUN Your **post** is the letters and packages that are delivered to you.
	railway (UK) / railroad (US)	NOUN A **railway** is a route between two places along which trains travel on steel rails.
	term (UK) / semester (US)	NOUN A **term** is one of the periods of time that a school, college, or university divides the year into.
	tick (UK) / check (US)	NOUN A **tick** is a written mark like a V: √. It is used to show that something is correct or has been selected or dealt with.
	underground, tube (UK) / subway (US)	NOUN The **underground** in a city is the railway system in which electric trains travel below the ground in tunnels.

Exercise 1

Write the missing words in sentence B so that it means the same as sentence A, as shown. Use American English.

1. **A** Unfortunately, the lift was out of order.
   B Sadly, the ___*elevator*___ wasn't working.
2. **A** I used my mobile to tell Roger I would be late.
   B I called Roger on my _____ to tell him I would be late.
3. **A** It's a long time till dinner. Would you like a biscuit?
   B Can I get you a _____, as we aren't going to have dinner for quite some time?
4. **A** It was a long film, so there was an interval halfway through.
   B The movie was so long there was an _____ halfway through.

Exercise 2

Choose the correct British English word, as shown.

1. My daughter-in-law is soon going to start her next **semester / (term)** at university.
2. The extended family travelled all the way there on the **underground / subway**.
3. Children, don't walk in the road. Stay on the **sidewalk / pavement**.
4. The building of the new **railroad / railway** has provided numerous jobs locally.
5. We went out during the **interval / intermission** to purchase some refreshments.
6. Jim had some coffee and **cookies / biscuits** during the morning.

Exercise 3

Find the words or phrases that are American English, as shown.

1 Things to eat	chips	French fries	crisps
2 Places to live	flat	house	apartment
3 Entertainment	movie	film	play
4 Urban places	city centre	downtown	town centre
5 Going away	holiday	vacation	break
6 Ways of travelling	railroad	tube	railway

Exercise 4

Put the correct British English word or phrase in each gap, as shown.

| city centre | crisps | interval | pavement | flat | post | ground floor | check |

1. first floor ___*ground floor*___
2. downtown _____
3. mail _____
4. sidewalk _____
5. potato chips _____
6. apartment _____

UNIT 1 British and American English words and phrases

Exercise 5
Write the British English equivalent of the American English word in brackets to complete each sentence, as shown.
1 When you complete the form, put a _____*tick*_____ (check) against the points you agree with.
2 This botanical garden is at its most splendid in the _____ (fall).
3 Last night, my cousins opted to go to the _____ (movie theatre), for a change.
4 Jasper had some _____ (fries) to go with the roast lamb he'd ordered.
5 Gemma had to take the _____ (elevator) to get to the penthouse on the top floor.
6 We've been working extremely hard all year, so it's time we took a _____ (vacation).

Exercise 6
For each question, tick the British word that means the same as the American word in italics, as shown.
1 I live in a large *apartment*.
   ❏ house
   ❏ cottage
   ☑ flat
2 My office is on the *first floor*.
   ❏ ground floor
   ❏ second floor
   ❏ basement
3 Walk on the *sidewalk*, not in the road.
   ❏ path
   ❏ pavement
   ❏ track
4 We start the next academic *semester* in September.
   ❏ period
   ❏ holiday
   ❏ term
5 I'll ask the waiter for the *check*.
   ❏ menu
   ❏ order
   ❏ bill
6 We can get into the city on the *subway*.
   ❏ bus
   ❏ underground
   ❏ tram

2 Entertainment and the media

Hot stuff for Mitcham

The desert sands of North Africa provide the **setting** for Danielle Mitcham's latest movie *The Proud Englishman*. The **plot**, which is based on the **classic** novel by Eric Jones, centres around a lonely English writer living in Algeria, who strikes up an unexpected friendship with a local boy. The **cast**, including Jed McIntosh as Jones, makes the most of a sensitive **script**, and the stylish **soundtrack** emphasizes the emotional story.

Look at one reader's review of the *Daily News*.

> I read the *Daily News* every day. It's my favourite newspaper, mainly because the sports **coverage** is fantastic. I think the **editor** does a good job of making sure that the news is presented in a way that is fair but interesting. I usually read what the music **critics** have to say about new albums and gigs. I especially like Nina French, whose articles are always highly **entertaining**.

Word Finder

applause	NOUN	**Applause** is the noise made by a group of people clapping their hands to show approval.
artistic		1 ADJECTIVE Someone who is **artistic** is good at drawing or painting, or arranging things in a beautiful way. 2 ADJECTIVE **Artistic** means relating to art or artists.
bestseller	NOUN	A **bestseller** is a book of which a great number of copies have been sold.
capture	VERB	If an event is **captured** in a photograph or on film, it is photographed or filmed.
cast	NOUN	The **cast** of a play or film is all the people who act in it.
classic	ADJECTIVE	A **classic** film, piece of writing, or piece of music is of very high quality and has become a standard against which similar things are judged.
compose	VERB	When someone **composes** a piece of music, they write it.
composer	NOUN	A **composer** is a person who writes music, especially classical music.

14 **Work on your Vocabulary** Upper Intermediate (B2)

UNIT 2 Entertainment and the media

conductor	NOUN A **conductor** is a person who stands in front of an orchestra or choir and directs its performance.
costume	NOUN An actor's or performer's **costume** is the set of clothes they wear while they are performing.
coverage	NOUN The **coverage** of something in the news is the reporting of it.
critic	NOUN A **critic** is a person who writes about and expresses opinions about things such as books, films, music, or art.
editor	NOUN An **editor** is a person who checks and corrects texts before they are published.
entertaining	ADJECTIVE If something is **entertaining**, it amuses or interests you and gives you pleasure.
episode	NOUN An **episode** of something, such as a series on radio or television or a story in a magazine, is one of the separate parts in which it is broadcast or published.
lyrics	NOUN The **lyrics** of a song are its words.
plot	NOUN The **plot** of a film, novel, or play is the connected series of events that make up the story.
script	NOUN The **script** of a play, film, or television programme is the written version of it.
setting	NOUN The **setting** of a film, book, etc., is where it takes place.
soundtrack	NOUN The **soundtrack** of a film is its sound, speech, and especially its music.

Exercise 1

Put the correct word in each gap.

lyrics | editor | conductor | soundtrack | episode | bestseller | coverage | critic

1 film _____
2 fiction _____
3 newspaper _____ _____ _____
4 television drama _____
5 stage musical _____ _____

Exercise 2

Which sentences are correct?

1 I enjoy painting and I'm thinking of going to artistic college when I leave school. ☑
2 The photographer spent a long time trying to capture the effect of the light shining through the autumn leaves. ☐
3 None of my friends enjoys classic music, but I quite like composers such as Mozart. ☐
4 I've heard that people enjoy costume dramas more when the economy is bad, perhaps because they offer an escape from present reality. ☐
5 The play had a very bad critic in the press, but nevertheless it was a popular success. ☐
6 It's a very entertaining film, just the thing to watch if you want to relax. ☐

Exercise 3
Put the correct word in each gap.

| plots | episodes | lyrics | composer | applause | cast | conductor |

Hi Aziza

We're having a great time in London. On Saturday we went to a West End musical and I felt that the ¹_____ was excellent. Some of them were people I'd seen acting in various ²_____ of TV soaps, but I'd no idea they could sing too. And the sound was brilliant, you could hear every word of the song ³_____.

At the end there was a surprise because when the ⁴_____ died down, the ⁵_____ left the orchestra, came up on stage and announced that the ⁶_____ of all the music was in the theatre that night. Then she came up and everyone cheered her.

Anyway, I'll tell you more when I see you.

Shahla

xxx

Exercise 4
Are the highlighted words correct or incorrect in the sentences?
1. The thunderous **applause** ☑ lasted for nearly ten minutes.
2. The novelist left the **episode** ☐ of what was supposed to be his next bestseller in a taxi.
3. The director and the whole **cast** ☐ were pleased with that day's filming.
4. In a long career, he **composed** ☐ the lyrics for over 20 hit musicals.
5. The original **setting** ☐ of the opera was seventeenth-century Rome, but they changed it to contemporary New York, which was weird.
6. We left the theatre halfway through the play because some of the actors hadn't learnt the **soundtrack** ☐ and the other half couldn't act.

Exercise 5
Choose the correct word.

Inheritance is the latest ¹**costume / dress** drama from FBC television.

The ²**scenery / setting** is nineteenth-century France, and according to most of the ³**critics / editors**, the team at FBC have another success on their hands. However, the ⁴**plot / script**, which concerns love and betrayal in a provincial town, is based on a short story and I thought it was a bit thin.

Nevertheless, it is very pretty to look at and there are some amusing ⁵**series / episodes**. To my ears, much of the music was too modern, but I guess that's what's known as ⁶**artistic / soundtrack** licence!

3

Places and buildings

Dear Mum
We're staying in a fantastic **resort** in Corsica. We've done some lovely walks along the **cliffs**, and visited most of the local **landmarks**. The hotel is in an amazing **location** near the sea. Our room has a great view, so every evening we sit on the balcony and watch the sun sinking over the **horizon** – bliss!
See you soon
Megan

Jane Webber
15 Southsea Walk
Upper Balsham
UK

I live in a **residential area** on the **outskirts** of Birmingham. The company where I work is based on an **industrial estate**, in another town about 30 miles away. It's not too bad getting to work, because it's **dual carriageway** most of the way. My wife works in the centre of Birmingham. She usually catches the bus to work because her company doesn't have a car park. There's a **multistorey** car park nearby, but it's very expensive.

Word Finder

ATM	NOUN An **ATM** is a machine built into the wall of a bank or other building, which allows people to take out money from their bank account by using a special card.
bay	NOUN A **bay** is a partly enclosed area, inside or outside a building, that is used for a particular purpose.
bistro	NOUN A **bistro** is a small, informal restaurant or a bar where food is served.
cashpoint	NOUN A **cashpoint** is a machine built into the wall of a bank or other building, which allows people to take out money from their bank account by using a special card.
cliff	NOUN A **cliff** is a high area of land with a very steep side, especially one next to the sea.
dual carriageway	NOUN A **dual carriageway** is a road that has two lanes of traffic travelling in each direction with a strip of grass or concrete down the middle to separate the two lots of traffic.
hardware store	NOUN A **hardware store** is a shop where articles for the house and garden such as tools, nails, and pans are sold.

17

horizon	NOUN The **horizon** is the line in the far distance where the sky seems to meet the land or the sea.
hostel	NOUN A **hostel** is a place where people can stay cheaply.
industrial estate	NOUN An **industrial estate** is an area that has been specially planned for a lot of factories.
landmark	NOUN A **landmark** is a building or feature that is easily noticed and can be used to judge your position or the position of other buildings or features.
location	NOUN A **location** is the place where something happens or is situated.
multistorey	ADJECTIVE A **multistorey** car park is a car park that has several floors.
one-way street	NOUN A **one-way street** is a road or street in which you are only allowed to drive in one direction.
opera house	NOUN An **opera house** is a theatre that is specially designed for the performance of operas.
outskirts	NOUN The **outskirts** of a city or town are the parts of it that are farthest away from its centre.
residential area	NOUN A **residential area** in a city is an area where many people live, rather than an area of business.
resort	NOUN A **resort** is a place where a lot of people spend their holidays.
skyline	NOUN The **skyline** is the line or shape that is formed where the sky meets buildings or the land.
suburbs	NOUN The **suburbs** of a city are areas where people live that are outside the centre of the city.

Exercise 1

Match the two parts.

1. Hey, Matt, have you got any money you can lend me?
2. I don't think we should be driving down this road. All the parked cars are pointing the other way!
3. Do you know why Linda was stopped by the police?
4. Where is the football club where you play?
5. Jack, I can't find the car, where did you park it?
6. You have changed all the door handles! These are so pretty.

a. You are right. It's a one-way street!
b. It's your lucky day, I've just been to the ATM.
c. In bay 27 on the sixth floor of the multistorey car park.
d. Yes, I bought them at the hardware store in town.
e. She was driving too fast down the dual carriageway.
f. On the outskirts of town, so I have to catch the bus.

18 **Work on your Vocabulary** Upper Intermediate (B2)

UNIT 3 Places and buildings

Exercise 2

For each question, tick the correct answer.

1 Where can you go if you want to have an inexpensive meal?
   - [ ] a restaurant
   - [ ] a coffee shop
   - [ ] a bistro

2 Which of the following can you buy in a hardware store?
   - [ ] hammer and nails
   - [ ] pens and paper
   - [ ] milk and bread

3 A tall building that you can see from a long way away can be called
   - [ ] the horizon.
   - [ ] a location.
   - [ ] a landmark.

4 A suburb is an area just outside the city where you can find
   - [ ] a lot of pollution.
   - [ ] much traffic.
   - [ ] many homes.

5 A hostel is a place where
   - [ ] students can stay cheaply.
   - [ ] people can go on holiday.
   - [ ] managers entertain their clients.

Exercise 3

Rearrange the letters to find words, as shown. Use the definitions to help you.

1 ldsntrauii eeatts ___*industrial estate*___ (an area outside town where you can find factories and other businesses)

2 dssaeei rsoter _____ (a place by the sea where people can go to relax and have a holiday)

3 yleinks _____ (the outline of the buildings in a city that you can see against the sky)

4 nkmaalrd _____ (a building or a place that you can recognize easily)

5 anolitco _____ (the place where something can be found)

6 ncpiahtso _____ (a machine, usually in the wall of a bank, where you can get money from your account)

Exercise 4
Complete the sentences by writing one word in each gap.
1 Ben, I can't find the _____ of that restaurant you told me about on this map. Where is it again?
2 For my birthday, we went to the opera _____ in Sydney and watched a wonderful Italian opera.
3 The dual _____ from here to Brighton is being expanded so that there will be three lanes instead of two.
4 I have always wanted to live on the _____ of town, so I would have views of the fields and the countryside from my windows.
5 The [a]_____ of cities have often been seen as ideal [b]_____ areas, but in fact they are not very convenient for getting into the city.
6 New York is famous for its wonderful _____, with all those tall towers rising into the blue.

Exercise 5
Which sentences are correct?
1 I made a mistake and drove the wrong way down a one-way street, nearly crashing the car. ❏
2 The suburbs where I live are full of shops, restaurants and office buildings. ❏
3 The opera house is a wonderful place for children, where they can play and use all the toys and games provided especially for them. ❏
4 The ATMs in this neighbourhood are all broken, because violent thieves try to get money out of them. ❏
5 If you look straight up into the sky at night, you will be able to see the moon, the stars and the horizon. ❏
6 I am sure I left the car in bay 14 on the third floor, so I have either forgotten the bay number or got the wrong floor in this multistorey car park. ❏
7 The holiday resorts in the north-east of Spain are particularly suitable for young families, with all the facilities you would want to keep everyone entertained on holiday. ❏

4 Relationships

I had a rather unusual **upbringing**. My parents **separated** when I was eight, and I went to live with my mum and her new husband. My **stepfather** was a wildlife photographer. He worked all over the world, and we went with him.

I think it was quite difficult for my mum to **raise** a child in those circumstances. We were often in very remote places, and she had to teach me herself, but they **stuck together** and we all had some great adventures.

When I was a student, my **roommate** Stacy had a brother who used to visit her from time to time. I always **fancied** him, but he didn't seem to notice me. When Stacy told me he'd **proposed** to his girlfriend, it nearly **broke my heart**.

However, now I think I had a lucky escape! He was a fairly successful actor, and their wedding was in all the papers. But Stacy says he has never been **faithful** to his wife, and everyone in the acting industry knows that he **cheats** on her. So far, his wife has **stood by** him, but Stacy says she's very unhappy.

Good to know!

To form the plural of words ending -in-law, put an s on the first part of the word:

brothers-in-law, mothers-in-law

Word Finder

adoption	NOUN **Adoption** is when someone legally becomes the parent of someone else's child.
ancestor	NOUN Your **ancestors** are the people from whom you are descended.
break someone's heart	PHRASE If you **break someone's heart**, you make them very unhappy because they love you and you do not love them.
brother-in-law / sister-in-law	NOUN Your **brother-in-law** is the brother of your husband or wife, or the husband of your sister. Your **sister-in-law** is the sister of your husband or wife, or the wife of your brother.
circle	NOUN Your **circle** of friends is your group of friends.
faithful	ADJECTIVE Someone who is **faithful** to their husband, wife, or lover does not have a sexual relationship with anyone else.
fancy	VERB If you **fancy** someone, you are attracted to them.

Word Finder

funeral	NOUN A **funeral** is the ceremony that is held when the body of someone who has died is buried or cremated.
propose	VERB If you **propose** to someone, you ask them to marry you.
proposal	NOUN A **proposal** is when someone asks someone to marry them.
raise	VERB Someone who **raises** a child looks after it until it is grown up.
roommate	NOUN Someone's **roommate** is a person they share a room, apartment, or house with, for instance when they are students.
separate	VERB If a couple who are married or living together **separate**, they decide to live apart.
stand by	PHRASAL VERB If you **stand by** someone, you continue to support them and be loyal to them.
stepmother / stepfather	NOUN Your **stepmother** is a woman who has married your father after the death or divorce of your mother. Your **stepfather** is a man who has married your mother after the death or divorce of your father.
stick together	PHRASAL VERB If two people **stick together**, they stay in their relationship.
take after	PHRASAL VERB If you **take after** an older person in your family, you are like them.
united	ADJECTIVE If people are **united**, they agree with each other and act together.
upbringing	NOUN Your **upbringing** is the way that your parents treat you and the things that they teach you when you are growing up.
widow	NOUN A **widow** is a woman whose husband has died.

Exercise 1

Complete the sentences by writing one word in each gap.

proposal | adoption | upbringing | stepmother | circle | ancestor | funeral | widow

1 It's good to have a wide _____ of friends, particularly when you need support through difficult times.
2 Although they had only known each other for a couple of months, Jane had no hesitation in accepting Darren's _____ and they got married the following month.
3 Barry's _____ was rather unconventional, as his parents moved from one country to another, so he never settled into one place.
4 Jemima and Laurence were surprised when research into their family trees revealed that they had a common _____.
5 Mrs Elkins had lived alone since becoming a _____ on the unexpected death of her husband.
6 Unlike the heroines of many children's stories, Mandy got on well with her _____, and was delighted that the marriage had made her father happy again.

22 **Work on your Vocabulary** Upper Intermediate (B2)

UNIT 4 Relationships

Exercise 2
Match the two parts.

1 cheat on someone
2 fancy someone
3 raise someone
4 stand by someone
5 stick together
6 take after someone

a to feel sexually attracted to someone
b to be similar to a member of your family in your appearance, your behaviour or your character
c to stay with someone and support them
d to look after a child until it is grown up
e to continue to give someone support, especially when they are in trouble
f to have a sexual relationship with a person who is not your husband, wife or usual partner

Exercise 3
Match the sentence halves.

1 My sister and brother-in-law are considering adoption, as
2 Most of my ancestors
3 You take after your mother's side of the family,
4 She had a very strict upbringing,
5 He was faithful
6 They tried hard to appear united

a they can't have children of their own.
b with your dark hair and olive skin.
c as a couple, but there were serious problems in the relationship.
d with parents who wouldn't let her speak at the table.
e came from that part of Ireland.
f to his wife throughout their 30-year marriage.

Exercise 4
Complete the sentences by writing one word in each gap.

| stand | cheating | break | stick | propose | fancy |

1 I think Mike's a really nice guy, but I don't _____ him.
2 Charles had booked a table in a really nice restaurant and I had a feeling he might _____ to me.
3 I think it would _____ his heart if Louisa left him.
4 When the papers published details of Taylor's affair with a much younger woman, his wife decided to _____ by her man.
5 Of course you go through difficult times as a family, but you have to _____ together.
6 If I found out Brendan was _____ on me, I'd end the relationship.

23

5

Beliefs and ideas

I've never been a **religious** person, but I find **theology** an extremely interesting subject. Obviously, there are many intelligent people who are **convinced** that God exists, and for whom the teachings of the Bible or the Koran influence the **morals** they live by. Everyone has a right to their own **beliefs** and I try not to be **narrow-minded** about it.

If everyone had to study **philosophy** at school, I believe the world would be a better place. Children are born **open-minded**, and we should try to **nurture** this characteristic. When people **maintain** a set of **beliefs** simply because that is what their parents told them, or what the church told them, it prevents their minds from working freely. Because philosophy can make us challenge our own beliefs, it can also make us more **tolerant** of the beliefs of others.

as far as I know	PHRASE	**As far as I know** is used to say that you believe that something is true but are not completely sure.
belief	NOUN	Your religious or political **beliefs** are your views on religious or political matters.
change your mind	PHRASE	If you **change your mind**, you change your opinion about something.
civilization	NOUN	A **civilization** is a society with its own social organization and culture.
convinced	ADJECTIVE	If you are **convinced** about something, you are sure that it is true.
credible	ADJECTIVE	**Credible** means able to be trusted or believed.
disbelieve	VERB	If you **disbelieve** someone or disbelieve something that they say, you do not believe that what they say is true.
legend	NOUN	A **legend** is a very old and popular story that may be true.
maintain	VERB	If you **maintain** something, you continue to have it, and do not let it stop or grow weaker.
moral	NOUN	**Morals** are principles and beliefs concerning right and wrong behaviour.
myth	NOUN	A **myth** is a well-known story that was made up in the past to explain natural events or to justify religious beliefs or social customs.
narrow-minded	ADJECTIVE	If you describe someone as **narrow-minded**, you are criticizing them because they are unwilling to consider new ideas or other people's opinions.

UNIT 5 Beliefs and ideas

Word Finder

nurture	VERB If you **nurture** plans, ideas, beliefs, or people, you encourage them or help them to develop.
open-minded	ADJECTIVE If you describe someone as **open-minded**, you approve of them because they are willing to listen to and consider other people's ideas and suggestions.
philosophy	NOUN **Philosophy** is the study or creation of theories about basic things such as the nature of existence, knowledge, and thought, or about how people should live.
religious	1 ADJECTIVE You use **religious** to describe things that are connected with religion or with one particular religion. 2 ADJECTIVE Someone who is **religious** has a strong belief in a god or gods.
ritual	NOUN A **ritual** is a religious service or other ceremony that involves a series of actions performed in a fixed order.
superstition	NOUN **Superstition** is belief in things that are not real or possible, for example magic.
theology	NOUN **Theology** is the study of the nature of God and of religion and religious beliefs.
tolerant	ADJECTIVE If you describe someone as **tolerant**, you approve of the fact that they allow other people to say and do as they like, even if they do not agree with or like it.

Exercise 1

Are the highlighted words correct or incorrect in the sentences?

1 A **superstition** ☐ is a belief that can be backed up by firm evidence.
2 I must admit I'm very **tolerant** ☐ and other people often get on my nerves.
3 My **philosophy** ☐ in life is 'live and let live'.
4 Mick's going to study **theology** ☐ and become a priest.
5 Karen's a pretty **open-minded** ☐ person – she can't understand other people's viewpoints.
6 I'm quite a **religious** ☐ person and my faith is very important to me.

Exercise 2

Rearrange the letters to find words. Use the definitions to help you.

1 viiiiztncoal _____ (human society)
2 smarlo _____ (beliefs about right and wrong)
3 thmy _____ (an ancient story that isn't true)
4 ltruai _____ (an activity that is repeated regularly and always done in the same way, often religious)
5 fbeeil _____ (an idea that you think is true)
6 hhppliosyo _____ (a way of thinking about life)

Exercise 3

Match the sentence halves.

1 As far as I know, Pippa
2 I've just written a book
3 I think people ought to read all they can about it
4 I've changed my mind
5 Fatima's convinced that
6 It's important to nurture

a is studying history, but I'm not 100% sure.
b her opinions are right.
c before deciding whether they believe or disbelieve in a religion.
d about certain issues recently.
e about ancient myths and legends.
f a sense of morality.

Exercise 4

Decide if the pairs of sentences have the same meaning.

1 A I have a morning ritual that includes reading the paper and drinking coffee.
  B If I don't read the paper and drink coffee in the morning, I don't feel good.
2 A She maintains her point of view even though there's evidence against it.
  B She hasn't changed her opinion, although evidence suggests it's incorrect.
3 A I'm fairly open-minded when it comes to religious beliefs.
  B I believe religion should be accessible to everyone.
4 A I don't think the story is very credible.
  B I don't really believe that story.
5 A Bethany is very narrow-minded when it comes to other people's opinions.
  B Bethany can't see other people's points of view.

Exercise 5

Complete the sentences by writing one word in each gap, as shown.

1 If you are _____*religious*_____ you have a strong belief in a particular religion.
2 A _____ is a system of beliefs and values about life.
3 A _____ is a society that is socially developed.
4 If you _____ something, you encourage it to grow.
5 _____ is the study of religion.
6 A _____ is a belief that is not based on evidence or logic.

Social and political issues

Rosa Knight
• READY TO WORK FOR YOU! •

Dear friends

As you know, the **council** elections are on April 4th. I hope you will elect me as your independent **councillor**!

I have lived in this area for many years, and am an active member of the **community**, running the local youth club and organizing the 'Save our Library' campaign.

I believe that national and local **government policies** are threatening our vibrant, **multicultural** community, and I want to fight back! At times like this, when our **economy** is struggling, it is important that we do everything we can to support those who are suffering.

If you elect me, I promise to cut **bureaucracy**, and fight for services that **benefit** everyone!

Vote Rosa Knight on April 4th to make a real difference for you!

Unfortunately, our **nation** is still divided into rich and poor. In our cities, **wealthy** people are driven around in big cars while beggars sleep in the streets.

Poverty is seen as a fact of life, rather than as the shameful thing it is, and nobody with the political power to achieve it cares about providing even the most basic **welfare** system.

Although in theory we have **democracy** in our country, in reality our **parliament** is run by a group of out-of-touch businessmen and army officials, who do not care about the majority of our citizens.

Words for social and political issues

	ballot	NOUN A **ballot** is a secret vote in which people select a candidate in an election, or express their opinion about something.
	benefit	VERB If you **benefit** from something or if it **benefits** you, it helps you or improves your life.
	bureaucracy	NOUN **Bureaucracy** refers to all the rules and procedures followed by government departments and similar organizations, especially when you think that these are complicated and cause long delays.
	citizen	NOUN Someone who is a **citizen** of a particular country is legally accepted as belonging to that country.
	community	NOUN The **community** is all the people who live in a particular area or place.
	consumer	NOUN A **consumer** is a person who buys things or uses services.
	consumerism	NOUN **Consumerism** is the belief that it is good to buy and use a lot of goods.
	contribute	VERB If you **contribute** to something, you say or do things to help to make it successful.
	council	NOUN A **council** is a group of people who are elected to govern a local area such as a city or, in Britain, a county.
	councillor	NOUN A **councillor** is a member of a council.
	democracy	NOUN **Democracy** is a system of government in which people choose their rulers by voting for them in elections.
	economics	NOUN **Economics** is the study of the way in which money, industry, and trade are organized in a society.
	economy	NOUN An **economy** is the system according to which the money, industry, and trade of a country or region are organized.
	govern	VERB To **govern** a country means to be officially in charge of it, and to have responsibility for making laws, managing the economy, and controlling public services.
	government	NOUN The **government** of a country is the group of people who are responsible for running it.
	lifestyle	NOUN The **lifestyle** of a particular person or group of people is the living conditions, behaviour, and habits that are typical of them or are chosen by them.
	multicultural	ADJECTIVE **Multicultural** means consisting of or relating to people of many different nationalities and cultures.
	nation	NOUN A **nation** is an individual country considered together with its social and political structures.
	national	ADJECTIVE **National** means relating to the whole of a country or nation rather than to part of it or to other nations.
	nationality	NOUN If you have the **nationality** of a particular country, you were born there or have the legal right to be a citizen.
	parliament	NOUN The **parliament** of some countries, for example Britain, is the group of people who make or change its laws, and decide what policies the country should follow.

Work on your Vocabulary Upper Intermediate (B2)

UNIT 6 Social and political issues

Word Finder

policy	NOUN A **policy** is a set of ideas or plans that is used as a basis for making decisions, especially in politics, economics, or business.
poverty	NOUN **Poverty** is the state of being extremely poor.
refugee	NOUN **Refugees** are people who have been forced to leave their homes or their country, either because there is a war there or because of their political or religious beliefs.
wealth	NOUN **Wealth** is the possession of large amounts of money, property or other valuable things.
wealthy	ADJECTIVE Someone who is **wealthy** has a large amount of money, property, or valuable possessions.
welfare	ADJECTIVE **Welfare** services are provided to help with people's living conditions and financial problems.

Exercise 1

Match the sentence halves.

1. A refugee is
2. Poverty is
3. Welfare is
4. Democracy is
5. Bureaucracy is
6. A citizen is

a. a system that provides financial help for those in need.
b. a system of rules and processes used by a company or government.
c. someone who has a legal right to live in a country.
d. the condition of being very poor.
e. a system of government where people elect their leaders.
f. someone who has had to leave their country because of danger.

Exercise 2

Complete the sentences by writing one word in each gap.

community | benefit | nationality | economy | democracy | consumerism | poverty | bureaucracy

1. As people get older, they tend to start feeling the _____ of having contributed to a state welfare system.
2. Far too many people in the world still live in extreme _____, not even able to feed themselves adequately.
3. Living in a _____ means having equal opportunities and living in freedom – at least, in theory.
4. Asked about her _____, Helen replied that although technically she was British, she felt Canadian, having spent most of her life in Canada.
5. There was a strong sense of _____ in the village, so the project team found that everyone wanted to help in some way.
6. The vast increase in the range of goods on sale shows that _____ has really taken hold here since my last visit.

29

Exercise 3

Which sentences are correct?

1 A ballot is a voting process. A policy is a system of making new laws. ❑
2 A community is a group of people who live in the same area. Lifestyle is the way people live. ❑
3 A council is a group of people who govern a town or city. A councillor is someone who gives people advice about their problems. ❑
4 The economy is a system that relates to the way money and goods are used in a country. Economics is the study of money, trade and industry. ❑
5 A multicultural society includes people of different backgrounds. A nation is a country that does not allow immigration. ❑
6 Government is the method of ruling a country. Parliament is the group of people who make or change laws in a country. ❑

Exercise 4

Are the highlighted words correct or incorrect in the sentences?

1 '**Lifestyle**' ❑ refers to people's beliefs and attitudes.
2 I live in a **multicultural** ❑ society, which means people of different nationalities prefer not to mix.
3 A **welfare** ❑ system meets the basic living needs of people unable to provide for themselves.
4 **Parliament** ❑ will hold a debate on social issues this week.
5 I don't really understand the **economics** ❑ and what makes it stronger or weaker.
6 Changes will be made to public transport charges on a **national** ❑ level.
7 Some people criticize the welfare state because they say it discourages people from **contributing** ❑ to the economy.

Exercise 5

Complete the sentences by writing one word in each gap. The first letter has been filled in for you.

1 My uncle accumulated great w _____ running several highly successful businesses.
2 C _____ are becoming more demanding and expect good value for money.
3 The inhabitants of a particular town or city are known as its c _____.
4 The c _____ elections will take place next week to decide who will form the local government.
5 People who live in a d _____ are able to vote for the people they would like to represent them in parliament.
6 The r _____ crossed the border into the safety of a neighbouring country, away from the danger of their own.

7

Experiences

Dear Ms Harris

<u>Youth worker</u>

I am writing to apply for the above position. As you will see from my CV, I **graduated from** university last summer with a degree in psychology. I believe that this subject is **relevant** in many ways to the job of youth worker.

I have always wanted to work with young people. For the last three summers, I have worked on a summer camp in order to **gain experience**, and last year I **was promoted** to the position of team **leader**, running a team of six people and a varied programme of activities.

I believe that the main **strengths** I could bring to this job are a sense of fun, good communication **skills**, and a willingness to take on new **challenges**.

I very much hope you will consider my application, and look forward to hearing from you,

Yours sincerely

Luke Maidment

From: Helen Green
To: Kate Newbold
Subject: Coming home!

Hi Kate!

Do you know of any good jobs in Cardiff? I'm coming home!
I can't stand it here any longer. Everyone else in the company was **born and bred** within ten miles of the place, and I've never **felt accepted**. I thought I'd be able to **adapt to** their ways, but it's hard, because they haven't been at all **welcoming**.

Last week I decided I'd had enough, and I told my boss I was leaving. Apart from anything else, I don't think I'd ever be able to **get used to** this awful weather!

So, see you very soon!

Lots of love

Helen

Words for talking about experiences

adapt to	PHRASAL VERB	If you **adapt to** something, you change your ideas and behaviour in order to deal with it successfully.
born and bred	PHRASE	If you are **born and bred** in a place, you are born there and grow up there.
challenge	NOUN	A **challenge** is something new and difficult that requires great effort and determination.
explore	VERB	If you **explore** something, such as an opportunity, you think about it or try it.
feel accepted	PHRASE	If you **feel accepted**, you feel that people like you and are happy for you to be with them.
gain experience	PHRASE	If you **gain experience**, you get more knowledge or skill by doing a job or activity.
get used to	PHRASE	If you **get used to** something, you become familiar with it.
graduate from	PHRASAL VERB	In Britain, when a student **graduates from** university, they have successfully completed a degree course.
identity	NOUN	Your **identity** is who you are and the kind of person you believe yourself to be.
be influenced by	PHRASE	If you are **influenced by** something, it affects how you think or what you do.
leader	NOUN	The **leader** of a group of people or an organization is the person who is in control of it or in charge of it.
promote	VERB	If you are **promoted**, you are given a more senior job.
promotion	NOUN	If you get a **promotion**, you are given a more senior job.
relevant	ADJECTIVE	Something that is **relevant** to a situation or person is important or significant in that situation or to that person.
skills	NOUN	Someone's **skills** are the things they have learned to do well, for example in their job.
strengths	NOUN	Your **strengths** are the things that you are good at.
talented	ADJECTIVE	Someone who is **talented** has a natural ability to do something well.
upbringing	NOUN	Your **upbringing** is the way that your parents treat you and the things that they teach you when you are growing up.
weaknesses	NOUN	Your **weaknesses** are the things that you are not very good at.
welcoming	ADJECTIVE	If someone is **welcoming** or if they behave in a **welcoming** way, they are friendly to you when you arrive somewhere, so that you feel happy and accepted.
worthwhile	ADJECTIVE	If something is **worthwhile**, it is enjoyable or useful, and worth the time, money, or effort that is spent on it.

UNIT 7 Experiences

Exercise 1

Match the two parts.

1 Has Katie finished her university course yet?
2 Ben seems to be talented on the violin.
3 Well, John, how is your part-time job going?
4 How's retirement, Matt?
5 This young artist is very talented: just look at that canvas hanging over there.
6 That child is going to be a leader one day.

a I am gaining a lot of experience working in a busy office, Uncle Tim.
b He has been promoted to lead violinist in the orchestra.
c Yes, she is going to graduate from Leeds at the end of the month.
d He was influenced by Picasso, you know, and studied his work closely.
e Yes, look at the way she has organized everyone else in her play group.
f I haven't got used to being free to do whatever I want yet, but I'm sure I will do soon.

Exercise 2

Complete the sentences by writing one word in each gap.

1 I stayed with my best friend last week and her husband was very _____. I felt really at home in their house.
2 I would go for this job as an office manager but I am not sure that I have all the _____ experience. I mean, they want people management for one thing, and I have never done that.
3 You know, Jackie has always wanted to be a teacher. I think it gives her a sense of
   a_____: of who she is and what she stands for. It's a
   b_____ career and should give her lots of satisfaction.
4 When you are writing your CV, you could start with a list of all your
   a_____: you know, the things that you can do well. Remember, your CV should be b_____ to the job you are applying for.
5 David is just not ready to leave that job. He hasn't yet _____ all the opportunities for promotion it can offer.
6 Young people often feel under pressure to make a decision about a career. They should really start by considering their a_____ as well as their
   b_____, to see whether there is a particular path they are most suited to.

Exercise 3

Find the wrong or extra word in each sentence.

1 I love my new job and feel accepted throughout by the whole team.
2 David has always wanted to be complete promoted at work, but it is such a small office that there are no real opportunities there.
3 Journalists don't often reveal the identity from of their sources.
4 Sarah is very talented in. She is an excellent musician.
5 It's not worthwhile for learning all this geography. It's won't be useful in my future career.
6 The point you are making is not relevant in to this discussion, I'm afraid.

33

Exercise 4

Choose the correct word or phrase.

1 When making a decision on whether to go to university or get a job, most young people are **influenced / organized / prejudiced** by financial considerations.
2 Some animals are better able to **adapt / used / bred** to a new environment than others.
3 Changing careers is always a **test / task / challenge**, but right now in my life that's just what I need.
4 Ricki really likes her husband's parents: she feels **received / accepted / agreed** by them as a member of the family.
5 One of Derek's greatest **disadvantages / responsibilities / weaknesses** as a boss is that he wants everyone to like him, and that's just not possible, I'm afraid.
6 I know the new house is small, but we can't afford anything larger at the moment so you'll just have to get **used to / adapt to / born and bred in** it.

Exercise 5

For each question, tick the correct answer.

1 The way parents raise children is called their
   ❏ childhood.
   ❏ upbringing.
   ❏ identity.
2 If something is worthwhile, then it is
   ❏ of value, good to do or to have.
   ❏ worth a lot of money.
   ❏ very expensive to buy.
3 If you say someone was born and bred in Cambridge, it means that
   ❏ Cambridge is a good place to live and raise a family.
   ❏ they look like everyone else born in Cambridge.
   ❏ Cambridge is where they were born and where they grew up.
4 When you get a promotion at work, it means
   ❏ you are given a higher position, usually with a better salary.
   ❏ they have been advertising your products.
   ❏ extra work has been given to you to do.
5 When people talk about their strengths and weaknesses, they mean
   ❏ how physically strong they are and whether they need to go to the gym.
   ❏ the amount of money they earn is not enough and they should be paid more.
   ❏ the things they do well and the things they need to learn to do better.

8 News and current affairs

> The *Daily Truth* newspaper yesterday **hit the headlines** itself, when MPs demanded to know the identity of the unnamed **source** who leaked documents about sensitive Ministry of Defence contracts to the paper. The prime minister is said to be furious at yet more negative **coverage** of the government's handling of these contracts, and in particular an **editorial** which accused the defence minister of lying to parliament. The *Daily Truth* has issued a **press release** standing by its claims and refusing to name its source.

Look at the following common collocations for words in this unit:

*If a newspaper sells more copies, its **circulation increases**.*
*If something is written about a lot in newspapers, it **receives** a lot of **coverage**.*
*If you do something on time, you **meet** your **deadline**, and if you don't, you **miss** your **deadline**.*
*People **hold** a **press conference** or **issue** a **press release** to tell journalists about something.*
*If something or someone **attracts** a lot of **publicity**, they are written or talked about a lot.*

Word Finder

circulation	NOUN The **circulation** of a newspaper or magazine is the number of copies that are sold each time it is produced.
column	NOUN In a newspaper, a **column** is one of two or more vertical sections which are read downwards.
columnist	NOUN A **columnist** is a journalist who regularly writes a particular kind of article in a newspaper or magazine.
coverage	NOUN The **coverage** of something in the news is the reporting of it.
critic	NOUN A **critic** is a person who writes about and expresses opinions about things such as books, films, music, or art.
current affairs	NOUN If you refer to **current affairs**, you are referring to political events and problems in society that are discussed in newspapers, and on television and radio.
deadline	NOUN A **deadline** is a time or date before which a particular task must be finished or a particular thing must be done.
edit	VERB If you **edit** a text such as an article or a book, you correct and adapt it so that it is suitable for publishing.

editor	NOUN	The **editor** of a newspaper or magazine controls it and decides what should go in it.
editorial	NOUN	An **editorial** is an article in a newspaper which gives the opinion of the editor or owner on a topic or item of news.
exclusive	NOUN	An **exclusive** is an article or report that does not appear in any other newspaper or magazine.
feature	NOUN	A **feature** is a special article in a newspaper or magazine, or a special programme on radio or television.
go to press	PHRASE	If a newspaper or magazine **goes to press**, it starts being printed.
hit the headlines	PHRASE	If a story **hits the headlines**, it appears in newspapers.
leader	NOUN	A **leader** in a newspaper is a piece of writing that gives the editor's opinion on an important news item.
mass media	NOUN	The **mass media** refers to methods for giving news and information to large numbers of people, for example TV, radio and newspapers.
press conference	NOUN	A **press conference** is a meeting held by a famous or important person in which they answer journalists' questions.
press release	NOUN	A **press release** is a written statement about a matter of public interest that is given to the press by an organization concerned with the matter.
publicity	NOUN	**Publicity** is information or actions that are intended to attract the public's attention to someone or something.
source	NOUN	A **source** is a person or book that provides information for a news story or for a piece of research.

Exercise 1

Complete the sentences by writing one word in each gap.

1 Have you read Farzana's latest _____ in today's newspaper? As always, it is very funny.

2 Yesterday, the newspaper was late going to a_____ and so they didn't meet their b_____.

3 A good reporter never reveals the people who have helped him, his _____.

4 The _____ seem to have taken over our lives, with TV having the biggest influence on what people know and think.

5 The latest story to hit the _____ is about the number of young people who are out of work.

6 That _____ about the pop band who won that TV competition must have been difficult to get. They never give interviews.

7 That story about the prime minister was the _____ in last night's papers, but I didn't think it was important enough. He didn't say anything he hadn't said before.

Work on your Vocabulary Upper Intermediate (B2)

Exercise 2

For each question, tick the correct answer.

1 If a story hits the headlines, it means that
   ❏ the story has become really important.
   ❏ the headline is very good.
   ❏ the topic is not suitable.

2 A press release is
   ❏ when a newspaper sells lots of copies.
   ❏ an official statement from someone about a topic of interest.
   ❏ the time when newspapers are sent to the shops.

3 An exclusive is when
   ❏ the editor is the only person who writes the article.
   ❏ only one person is interviewed.
   ❏ the news story is available in only one newspaper.

4 Political or social stories that are happening at the moment are called
   ❏ features.
   ❏ editorials.
   ❏ current affairs.

5 TV, newspapers and the radio which provide information to the public are called
   ❏ publicity.
   ❏ mass media.
   ❏ circulation.

6 When someone in the news decides to meet journalists from different newspapers at the same time and answer their questions, it's called
   ❏ a press conference.
   ❏ going to press.
   ❏ coverage.

Exercise 3

Choose the correct word.

1 The report from our top journalist hadn't come in yet, but we couldn't wait any longer so we had to go to **press / publish / media** with what we had.
2 News about our economic problems is currently the **head / leader / top** in most newspapers.
3 Thomas Woods is a food **critic / criticism / critical** and has visited most of the restaurants in town.
4 Journalists try never to reveal their **helpers / colleagues / sources**, especially when these are people who often provide very useful information.
5 *Top News* newspaper has become very popular recently, with a **movement / circulation / production** of over two million papers per week.

Exercise 4

Rearrange the letters to find words. Use the definitions to help you.

1. iiotdlrea _____ (the article in a newspaper which gives the editor's views on a topic)
2. eednidla _____ (the time or date that completed work must be submitted)
3. uciytbpil _____ (when the media focuses attention on someone or something)
4. tedi _____ (checking something to get it ready for publishing or printing)
5. geaorvce _____ (how the media reports on news, an issue or a problem)
6. nulmoc _____ (a regular article in a newspaper that deals with the same issue or is written by the same journalist each time)

Exercise 5

Which sentences are correct?

1. Jack Nichols wrote an exclusive about the Queen which had appeared many times before. ❑
2. Marian Jones is a columnist who writes regularly about education. ❑
3. The person with the most responsibility in a newspaper is the editor, because he or she has the final say in all the decisions. ❑
4. This news story has had a lot of circulation, because all the newspapers have an article about it. ❑
5. The prime minister has had a meeting with all his ministers and everyone is waiting for the latest current affairs about it. ❑
6. The new department store in town has had a lot of publicity in the local newspapers. ❑

Exercise 6

Match the two parts together.

1	An editor is someone who	a	judges works of art, theatrical productions or even restaurants.
2	Circulation is	b	the number of copies of a newspaper or magazine sold to the public.
3	A columnist is someone who	c	is responsible for deciding what should go into a newspaper.
4	A press conference is	d	writes regularly for a newspaper.
5	A critic is someone who	e	a meeting at which an important person gives an interview to a lot of journalists.
6	A feature is	f	a story told in depth and detail in a newspaper or magazine.

9

The natural world

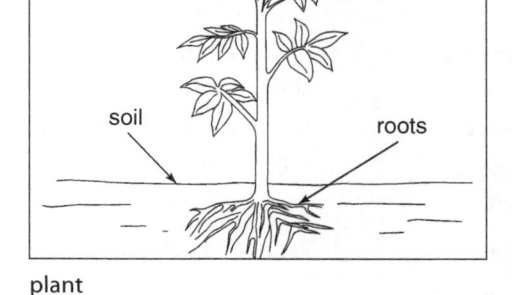

rainbow

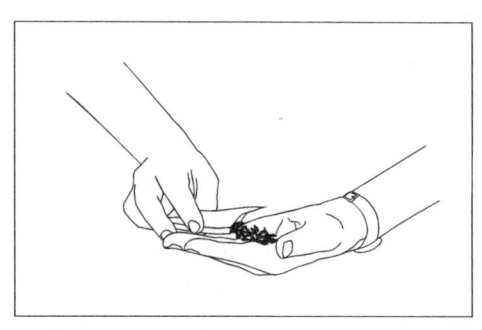

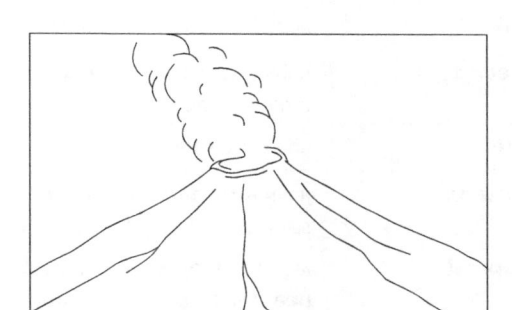

plant

seeds

volcano

Read about a group campaigning for the conservation of tropical areas.

> Our group campaigns for the **conservation** of **tropical** areas. We are particularly concerned about the protection of **endangered species**, both of animals and plants, and would like to see more nature **reserves** set up by governments in **rural** areas. The destruction of these areas for industry is a major cause of **global warming**, so we are also researching alternative methods of creating income for local people, such as the development of **ecological** tourism.

Word Finder	carbon footprint	NOUN Your **carbon footprint** is a measure of the amount of carbon dioxide released into the atmosphere by your activities over a particular period.
	carbon monoxide	NOUN **Carbon monoxide** is a poisonous gas that is produced especially by the engines of vehicles.
	carbon dioxide	NOUN **Carbon dioxide** is a gas produced by animals, by people breathing out and by chemical reactions.
	climate change	NOUN **Climate change** is the way the world's general weather conditions are changing.
	conservation	NOUN **Conservation** is saving and protecting the environment.
	ecological	ADJECTIVE **Ecological** means involved with or concerning ecology and the environment.
	endangered	ADJECTIVE If a species is **endangered**, it may die out.

39

evolution	NOUN	**Evolution** is a process of gradual change that takes place over many generations, during which species of animals, plants, or insects slowly change some of their physical characteristics.
global warming	NOUN	**Global warming** is the gradual rise in the earth's temperature caused by high levels of carbon dioxide and other gases in the atmosphere.
harvest	1 NOUN	The **harvest** is the gathering of a crop.
	2 NOUN	A **harvest** is the crop that is gathered in.
rainbow	NOUN	A **rainbow** is an arch of different colours that you can sometimes see in the sky when it is raining.
reserve	NOUN	A **reserve** is an area of land where the animals, birds, and plants are officially protected.
root	NOUN	The **roots** of a plant are the parts of it that grow under the ground.
rural	ADJECTIVE	**Rural** places are far away from large towns or cities.
seed	NOUN	A **seed** is the small, hard part of a plant from which a new plant grows.
soil	NOUN	**Soil** is the substance on the surface of the earth in which plants grow.
species	NOUN	A **species** is a class of plants or animals whose members have the same main characteristics and are able to breed with each other.
tide	NOUN	The **tide** is the regular change in the level of the sea on the shore.
tornado	NOUN	A **tornado** is a violent wind storm consisting of a tall column of air which spins round very fast and causes a lot of damage.
tropical	ADJECTIVE	**Tropical** means belonging to or typical of the parts of the world that are near the tropics (= two imaginary lines north and south of the equator).
volcano	NOUN	A **volcano** is a mountain from which hot melted rock, gas, steam, and ash from inside the Earth sometimes burst.

Exercise 1

Choose the correct word or phrase.

1 Incredibly, the farm is at the foot of **a living / an active / an energetic** volcano.
2 You can walk across to the island when the tide is **out / off / away**.
3 Crops grow well here, because the soil is so **mature / fertile / successful**.
4 The panda is now **a threatened / an insecure / an endangered** species.
5 Many of these people live in **rural / lonely / country** areas.
6 This kind of oil drilling is **an ecological / a geological / a geographical** disaster.

Exercise 2

Match the sentence halves.

1 We were able to walk right up to
2 Global warming is likely to lead to
3 The soil around the river
4 We found ourselves trapped in a small bay
5 The tornado was strong enough
6 This chart shows the different

a to lift vehicles into the air.
b is particularly fertile.
c when the tide came in.
d stages of human evolution.
e much of this land disappearing under the sea.
f the mouth of the volcano.

UNIT 9 The natural world

Exercise 3
Complete the sentences by writing the correct word or phrase in each gap.

| climate change | roots | reserve | harvests | carbon monoxide | carbon footprint |

1 Bad weather has led to poor _____ this year.
2 The area has been designated a wildlife _____.
3 The _____ of the oak trees are causing damage to our house.
4 We have installed solar panels in an attempt to reduce our _____.
5 Industry is a major contributor to _____.
6 These aircraft release large amounts of _____ into the atmosphere.

Exercise 4
Rearrange the letters to find words. Use the definitions to help you.

1 onaclov _____ (a mountain from which melted, hot rock sometimes erupts)
2 niouleovt _____ (the gradual process by which animals and plants change over many centuries)
3 boallg nigmraw _____ (the gradual rise in the earth's temperature)
4 wbniaro _____ (an arch of different colours made by the sun shining through drops of rain)
5 notroda _____ (a violent wind storm with a tall column of spinning air)
6 banroc prittfoon _____ (the amount of carbon dioxide that your daily activities cause to be released into the atmosphere)

Exercise 5
Put the correct word or phrase in each gap.

| harvests | species | seed | rural | conservation | climate change |

Coping with climate change

My job involves working with farmers, often in remote ¹_____ villages, to help them deal with the effects of ²_____. In some areas, ³_____ have been badly affected by changes in weather patterns.

Often, using different ⁴_____ of plants can make a huge difference and so we provide a variety of ⁵_____ samples for farmers to try. We also explain various methods of water ⁶_____, which can lead to higher levels of crop production.

10 Natural phenomena

> The president went on national TV last night to **express sympathy for** all those affected by the **blizzards** that swept across the country yesterday, doing enormous damage to homes and crops. The president called what happened a **'catastrophe'**, and promised an investigation into why no **evacuation** had been planned, despite warnings from weather experts. Local people are already hard at work trying to clear up the **debris**, and a fund has been set up to help **victims** who lost their homes and businesses. Six people are known to have died in the storms, and **rescue teams** are still searching for **survivors**.

	blizzard	NOUN A **blizzard** is a very heavy snowstorm with strong winds.
	bystander	NOUN A **bystander** is a person who is present when something happens and who sees it but does not take part in it.
	catastrophe	NOUN A **catastrophe** is an unexpected event that causes great suffering or damage.
	cut off	PHRASAL VERB If an area is **cut off**, it cannot be reached.
	debris	NOUN **Debris** is pieces from something that has been destroyed or pieces of rubbish or unwanted material that are spread around.
	demolish	VERB To **demolish** something such as a building means to destroy it completely.
	dig	VERB If people or animals **dig**, they make a hole in the ground or in a pile of earth, stones, or rubbish.
	eruption	NOUN An **eruption** is when a volcano throws out a lot of hot, melted rock and ash and steam.
	evacuation	NOUN An **evacuation** is when people have to leave their homes because of a danger such as flooding.
	famine	NOUN **Famine** is a situation in which large numbers of people have little or no food, and many of them die.
	glacier	NOUN A **glacier** is an extremely large mass of ice that moves very slowly, often down a mountain valley.
	heatwave	NOUN A **heatwave** is a period of time when the weather is much hotter than usual.

UNIT 10 Natural phenomena

Word Finder

rescue team	NOUN A **rescue team** is a group of people who try to rescue people, for instance in mountains.
search dog	NOUN A **search dog** is a dog that is trained to search for people.
shield	VERB If someone or something **shields** you from a danger or risk, it provides protection from it.
survivor	NOUN A **survivor** of a disaster, accident, or illness is someone who continues to live afterwards in spite of coming close to death.
submerged	ADJECTIVE If something is **submerged**, it is under water.
sympathy	NOUN If you feel **sympathy** for someone, you are sorry for the situation they are in.
trapped	ADJECTIVE If someone is **trapped**, they are stuck in a place.
victim	NOUN A **victim** is someone who has been hurt or killed.

Exercise 1

Rearrange the letters to find words. Use the definitions to help you.

1 darzilbz _____ (a very heavy snowstorm with strong winds)
2 rednaybst _____ (someone who is there when something happens but does not take part in it)
3 phesattacro _____ (an event that causes great suffering or damage)
4 nmafie _____ (a situation in which people suffer and die because there is not enough food)
5 ecalgir _____ (a large mass of ice that moves slowly)
6 aethevwa _____ (a period of very hot weather)

Exercise 2

Put the correct word or phrase in each gap.

| survivors | trapped | debris | demolishing | search dogs | shield |

Deadly storms hit southern states

Thousands of people rushed for shelter yesterday as fierce storms swept across the southern states, [1]_____ many homes and businesses. Rescue workers are using [2]_____ in a desperate attempt to locate those still [3]_____ under fallen buildings.

So far, two extremely lucky [4]_____ have been found inside a large metal cupboard which proved strong enough to [5]_____ them from the bricks falling around them. The Government has promised to send in the army to help clear up the [6]_____, which is scattered over hundreds of square miles.

Exercise 3

Choose the correct word or phrase.

1 Almost the entire village was **underwater / submerged / swept** by the floods.
2 The **eruption / evacuation / heatwave** sent huge clouds of ash into the sky.
3 Gale-force winds have **collapsed / exploded / demolished** many of the town's buildings.
4 Many of the affected areas are still **blocked / cut off / broken off** after flooding.
5 Several wounded people were **found / dug / evacuated** out from under the collapsed buildings yesterday.
6 The five **victims / sufferers / deaths** of last week's forest fires have been named.

Exercise 4

Match the sentence halves.

1 Forecast storms have led to
2 The President went on TV last night to express
3 Rescue teams have been searching for
4 The recent heatwave has led to an increase in people
5 Bystanders rushed to help as
6 It was not possible to drive that night

a survivors of this morning's earthquake.
b the evacuation of thousands of families.
c because of the blizzard conditions outside.
d children were swept into the sea.
e the nation's sympathy for the victims and their families.
f seeking medical attention for breathing difficulties.

Exercise 5

Complete the sentences by writing one word in each gap.

| famine | debris | blizzard | eruption | catastrophe | glacier |

1 What had started as light snow later turned into a _____.
2 Nobody was prepared for the volcano's _____.
3 These floods are a _____ for farmers.
4 Our homes had been reduced to piles of _____.
5 It is possible to ski on the _____, even in summer.
6 Food supplies have been sent in an attempt to ease the _____.

11 House and home

Is your current home too much for you now?

Why not move to a luxury **bungalow** on our beautiful retirement estate? Our **detached** homes are set in beautiful gardens which all our **residents** enjoy, and which are just one of the features that help everyone **settle** here so quickly. All the maintenance of the homes is done by us, and we can arrange any additional kind of **domestic** help you may require.

Until last year, I lived on a **houseboat**, but it was so cold in winter that I decided to move. I now have a **studio flat** in a **tower block** in the city centre. It's small, but so was the boat!

I paint, and I've **put up** several of my pictures, which is nice. The views I have looking over the city are great! It's pretty noisy in the daytime though, because there's a lot of **construction** work going on around here. More and more **high-rise** blocks, I expect!

Word Finder

atmosphere	NOUN The **atmosphere** of a place is the general impression that you get when you are in it.
bench	NOUN A **bench** is a long seat of wood or metal that two or more people can sit on.
bungalow	NOUN A **bungalow** is a house that has only one level, and no stairs.
cabinet	NOUN A **cabinet** is a cupboard used for storing things such as medicine or alcoholic drinks or for displaying decorative things in.
construction	NOUN **Construction** is the building of things such as houses, factories, roads, and bridges.
detached	ADJECTIVE A **detached** house is one that is not joined to any other house.
domestic	ADJECTIVE **Domestic** items and services are intended to be used in people's homes rather than in factories or offices.
high-rise	ADJECTIVE **High-rise** buildings are modern buildings that are very tall and have many levels or floors.
houseboat	NOUN A **houseboat** is a small boat on a river or canal that people live in.
hook	NOUN A **hook** is a bent piece of metal or plastic that is used for catching or holding things, or for hanging things up.

Word Finder

pull something down	PHRASAL VERB	If you **pull** a building **down**, you destroy it.
put something up	PHRASAL VERB	If you **put up** shelves, you attach them to the walls.
resident	NOUN	The **residents** of a house or area are the people who live there.
semi-detached	ADJECTIVE	A **semi-detached** house is a house that is joined to another house on one side by a shared wall.
settle	VERB	If you **settle** somewhere or settle in somewhere, you get used to being there and feel comfortable there.
shed	NOUN	A **shed** is a small building that is used for storing things such as garden tools.
storey	NOUN	A **storey** of a building is one of its different levels, which is situated above or below other levels.
studio flat	NOUN	A **studio flat** is a small flat, usually with one large room for cooking, sitting and sleeping in, and a separate bathroom.
terrace(d) house	NOUN	A **terraced house** or a **terrace house** is one of a row of similar houses joined together by their side walls.
tower block	NOUN	A **tower block** is a tall building divided into flats or offices.

Exercise 1

Write the missing word to complete each sentence. Use the clues in brackets to help you.

1 They redecorated their flat to give it a cosier _____ (a_ _ _ _ _ _ _ _).
2 The trouble with living on a _____ (h _ _ _ _ _ _ _) on the river is that it always feels damp.
3 If you get a furnished flat, it'll have all the _____ (d _ _ _ _ _ _) appliances you need.
4 Which _____ (s _ _ _ _ _) of the building do you live on?
5 How long did it take you to _____ (s _ _ _ _ _) down in your new neighbourhood?
6 Are you a _____ (r _ _ _ _ _ _ _) of the USA?

Exercise 2

Put the correct word in each gap.

| citizens | atmosphere | storey | construction |
| studio | bedroom | residents | domestic |

Flat to rent

Looking for a compact, affordable flat? Look no further! This ¹_____ flat in the city centre is available from April. The modern furniture and decoration give this flat a contemporary ²_____. It is well equipped with all new ³_____ appliances, e.g. dishwasher and washing machine. It's on the fifth floor of an eight- ⁴_____ building which has won a design award for its steel and glass ⁵_____. Most of the ⁶_____ are young professionals.

Work on your Vocabulary Upper Intermediate (B2)

UNIT 11 House and home

Exercise 3

Put the correct word or phrase in each gap.

| settled in | drawer | terraced | hook | pull down |
| cabinet | detached | put down | put up |

Hi Mike

I've just moved into a new house that I share with two other students. I had to move from my old flat, because they're going to ¹_____ the whole block. My new place is a ²_____ house and everyone told me it would be noisy, because I would be able to hear my neighbours on both sides, but it isn't a problem. I've ³_____ quickly because my housemates are really friendly. I've got a big room and I've ⁴_____ some extra shelves for my books. I just need a ⁵_____ on the back on the door for my coat and I might buy a bedside ⁶_____ to put my lamp on. When can you come and see my new place?

David

Exercise 4

Match the words with their definitions.

1 bench   a You can hang your coat on this.
2 hook   b This type of building is very tall.
3 cabinet   c This place has one room for sleeping and living in.
4 studio flat   d This is a type of cupboard.
5 houseboat   e You can live in this on a river.
6 high-rise   f You can sit on this in the park.

Exercise 5

Rearrange the letters to find words. Use the definitions to help you.

1 smharpeote _____ (the feeling in a place)
2 metdcois _____ (of the house, home or family)
3 yeorts _____ (level or floor in a building)
4 tusonoricnct _____ (building work)
5 tehdcade _____ (not connected to another building)
6 tinresed _____ (person who lives in a place)

47

Exercise 6

Match the words with the pictures.

1 bungalow

2 detached house

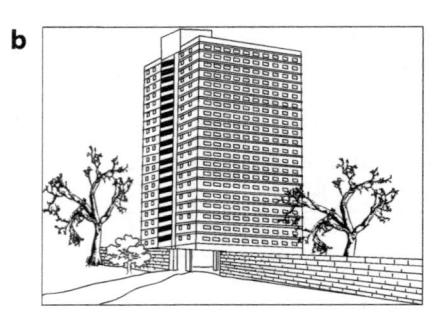

3 semi-detached house

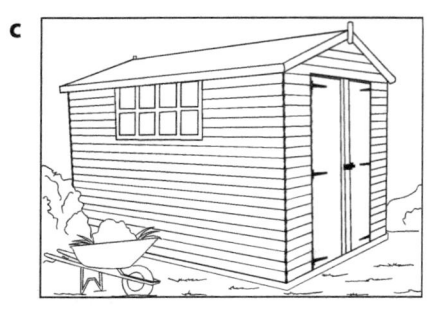

4 terraced house

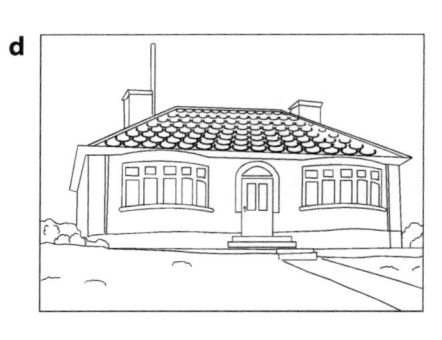

5 shed

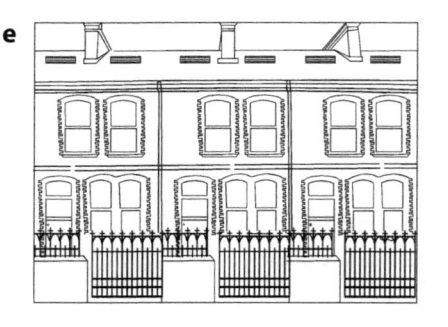

6 tower block

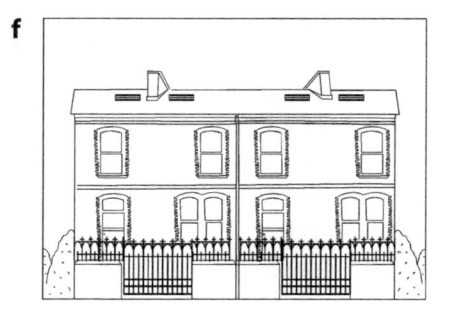

a

b

c

d

e

f

48 **Work on your Vocabulary** Upper Intermediate (B2)

12

Health, medicine and exercise

Doctor Good morning, Mr Goode. What can I do for you?

Mr Goode I haven't been feeling well for a couple of weeks. I have a **sore throat** and a **runny nose** all the time, but I don't really seem to have a cold. Also, my eyes are stinging.

Doctor I see. It may be that you have an **allergy**. They're very common at this time of year. Have you had a **rash** at all?

Mr Goode Yes, I had one on my stomach for a while, but it's gone now.

Doctor I expect that's what it is. I'll give you a **prescription** for that, and you could try using some **eye drops** to help your eyes. If you're not better in a week, come and see me again.

Last month, I fell off my bike and broke my wrist quite badly. I had an x-ray, and the doctor told me that I would need **surgery** to fix it properly. I had the operation a week later.

The **surgeon** came to the **ward** beforehand to discuss what he was going to do. I was only in hospital for a day. They sent me home with a **dose** of strong **painkillers**, and I had to go back a week later for the doctors to check the **wound**.

Word Finder

	AIDS	NOUN **AIDS** is a disease that destroys the natural system of protection that the body has against other diseases. AIDS is an abbreviation for 'acquired immune deficiency syndrome'.
	allergy	NOUN If you have a particular **allergy**, you become ill or get a rash when you eat, smell, or touch something that does not normally make people ill.
	antibiotics	NOUN **Antibiotics** are medical drugs used to kill bacteria and treat infections.
	blood pressure	NOUN Your **blood pressure** is the amount of force with which your blood flows around your body.
	bruise	NOUN A **bruise** is an injury that appears as a purple mark on your body, although the skin is not broken.
	cholesterol level	NOUN Your **cholesterol level** is the amount of the substance cholesterol (= a fatty substance that can cause heart disease if you have too much) that you have in your body.
	dose	NOUN A **dose** of medicine or a drug is a measured amount of it which is intended to be taken at one time.
	eye drops	NOUN **Eye drops** are a kind of medicine that you put in your eyes one drop at a time.
	injection	NOUN If you have an **injection**, a doctor or nurse puts a medicine into your body using a device with a needle called a syringe.

	painkiller	NOUN A **painkiller** is a type of medicine that reduces or stops pain.
	plaster	NOUN A **plaster** is a strip of sticky material used for covering small cuts or sores on your body.
	prescription	NOUN A **prescription** is the piece of paper on which your doctor writes an order for medicine and which you give to a chemist or pharmacist to get the medicine.
	pulse	NOUN Your **pulse** is the regular beating of blood through your body, which you can feel when you touch particular parts of your body, especially your wrist.
	rash	NOUN A **rash** is an area of red spots that appears on your skin when you are ill or have a bad reaction to something that you have eaten or touched.
	runny nose	NOUN If someone has a **runny nose**, liquid is coming from their nose, usually because they have a cold.
	sore throat	NOUN If someone has a **sore throat**, their throat hurts, often because they have an illness.
	surgeon	NOUN A **surgeon** is a doctor who is specially trained to perform surgery.
	surgery	NOUN **Surgery** is medical treatment in which someone's body is cut open so that a doctor can repair, remove, or replace a diseased or damaged part.
	ward	NOUN A **ward** is a room in a hospital that has beds for many people, often people who need similar treatment.
	wound	NOUN A **wound** is damage to part of your body, especially a cut or a hole in your flesh, which is caused by a gun, knife, or other weapon.

Exercise 1

Choose the correct word or phrase.

The company medical centre offers the following care for employees and their families:

Regular health checks, including, where appropriate, ¹**blood pressure / eye drops**.

The nurse can also take blood samples to monitor ²**pulse / cholesterol level**, etc.

She is qualified to write ³**prescriptions / injections** for medications such as ⁴**sore throats / antibiotics**, and can treat minor ⁵**wounds / wards** which do not require ⁶**surgery / doses**.

Exercise 2

Rearrange the letters to find words. Use the definitions to help you.

1 gylarel _____ (hay fever is one example of this)
2 busier _____ (a sign that you have knocked yourself against something hard)
3 trooshelcel velle _____ (a high-fat diet may raise this)
4 odes _____ (the amount of medication that is given to a particular person)
5 straple _____ (this is what you need when you cut your hand)
6 ungores _____ (this is a type of doctor who performs an operation)

UNIT 12 Health, medicine and exercise

Exercise 3
Which sentences are correct?
1. This laboratory has developed a number of drugs used in the treatment of patients with AIDS. ❑
2. I have allergy to all kinds of prawn and other shellfish, unfortunately. ❑
3. I think you should see the doctor instead of taking so much painkiller dose. ❑
4. You're looking very pale, let me look at your pulse. ❑
5. One symptom of this disease is a rash which may be itchy or painful. ❑
6. My brother is working on the maternity ward for six months, then he has more medical exams. ❑

Exercise 4
Are the highlighted words correct or incorrect in the sentences?
1. Many people do not understand that the widespread use of **antibiotics** ❑ can lead to all kinds of problems.
2. Modern equipment has made it possible for patients to monitor their own **blood pressure** ❑ regularly.
3. The doctor noticed a strange **bruise** ❑ mark on the man's leg.
4. I was told my condition did not require **surgery** ❑ at the moment, but it might be necessary in a few years' time.
5. This medicine is only available in **prescription** ❑ form, so you have to see a doctor to get it.
6. Can you help me? I've cut my finger and I need to **plaster** ❑ it.

Exercise 5
Are the highlighted words correct or incorrect in this text?

Dear Lizzie

Sorry I haven't been in touch recently, but I've been so busy. The whole family seems to have had one problem after another! James has just discovered he's ¹**allergy** ❑ to wheat. At first the doctor thought he had some infection so he was on ²**antibiotics** ❑, but that did no good, and after numerous trips to the GP's ³**surgery** ❑ we were finally referred to a specialist. Now James ⁴**doses** ❑ every morning, we're careful about what he eats and he's much better already.

Of course, there are lots of colds about with the beginning of the autumn term. Both the children are ⁵**runny noses** ❑ but haven't had to miss any school so far. Amazingly, I'm fine myself, but maybe it's only a matter of time – even the cat's been to the vet with a ⁶**rash** ❑ on her ear!

Anyway, that's enough about this family. How are you? Better than us, I hope!

Much love

Delia

13 Feelings

Ask Annabel

Dear Annabel
My problem is my four year-old son. Recently, he's become very **aggressive**. The slightest thing seems to **upset** him and then he starts screaming. My mother came to stay with us recently, and was **horrified** by his behaviour. I feel completely **helpless**. My son is clearly unhappy, but I don't know how to help him.

Laura, Manchester

Dear Laura
Poor you! You must be **exhausted** with trying to cope with your son. Please don't feel **guilty** – this sort of thing is more common than you think. I can give you details of some organizations that may be able to help. The main piece of advice I would give you is that you should create some simple but **fair** rules, and show your son that you are **determined** to be the boss!

Dear Annabel
Life with my girlfriend has been getting more and more **miserable** over the last few months. The problem is that she's so jealous. I'm a **sociable** kind of guy, but she gets **suspicious** even if I'm just texting my friends. It's driving me mad! We've been together for nearly four years, but it's difficult to be **optimistic** about our future together.

Ethan, Edinburgh

Dear Ethan
You have every right to feel **frustrated** with the situation. Have you tried talking to her? Can you tell her that you're **puzzled** about her lack of trust, and that it **hurts** you to know that she feels this way? Maybe she really is afraid of losing you, but if she carries on like this, she's got a **lonely** future ahead of her.

Word Finder

aggressive	ADJECTIVE	An **aggressive** person has a quality of anger and determination that makes them ready to attack other people.
determined	ADJECTIVE	If you are **determined** to do something, you have made a firm decision to do it and will not let anything stop you.
disgusting	ADJECTIVE	If you say that something is **disgusting**, you think it is extremely unpleasant or completely unacceptable.
exhausted	ADJECTIVE	If someone is **exhausted**, they are extremely tired.
fair	ADJECTIVE	Something or someone that is **fair** is reasonable, right, and just.
frustration	NOUN	**Frustration** is the feeling of being upset or angry because you are unable to do anything about a problem or bad situation.
guilty	ADJECTIVE	If you feel **guilty**, you feel unhappy because you think that you have done something wrong or have failed to do something that you should have done.
helpless	ADJECTIVE	If you are **helpless**, you do not have the strength or power to do anything useful or to control or protect yourself.
horrified	ADJECTIVE	If someone is **horrified**, they are very shocked and upset.

Work on your Vocabulary Upper Intermediate (B2)

UNIT 13 Feelings

Word Finder

hurt	VERB If someone **hurts** you or **hurts** your feelings, they say or do something that makes you unhappy.
lonely	ADJECTIVE Someone who is **lonely** is unhappy because they are alone or do not have anyone they can talk to.
miserable	ADJECTIVE If you are **miserable**, you are very unhappy.
optimistic	ADJECTIVE Someone who is **optimistic** is hopeful about the future or the success of something in particular.
pessimistic	ADJECTIVE Someone who is **pessimistic** thinks that bad things are going to happen.
pride	NOUN **Pride** is a feeling of satisfaction that you have because you or people close to you have done something good.
puzzled	ADJECTIVE Someone who is **puzzled** is confused because they do not understand something.
shocked	ADJECTIVE If someone is **shocked** by something, they are very surprised and often upset by it.
sociable	ADJECTIVE **Sociable** people are friendly and enjoy talking to other people.
suspicious	ADJECTIVE If you are **suspicious** of someone or something, you do not trust them, and are careful when dealing with them.
upset	VERB If something **upsets** you, it makes you feel worried or unhappy.

Exercise 1

Choose the correct word.

1 Why are you always **optimistic / pessimistic**? Things may turn out better than you expect.
2 That man was so **aggressive / exhausted** I thought he was going to hit me.
3 I'm absolutely **determined / frustrated** not to fail my driving test again.
4 What have you been up to? You're looking extremely **puzzled / guilty**.
5 I have to go and look after my brother. He's completely **helpless / shocked** since he broke his arm.
6 Did you say something mean to Judy? I'm sure you **upset / hurt** her feelings.

Exercise 2

Match the sentence halves.

1 No wonder Robert is always getting into fights
2 Paul always gives in
3 It's Bill's weekly battle to earn enough
4 Rupert is so inexperienced
5 Considering that Jake's job doesn't make use of his skills,
6 Steven obviously needs more help,

a but he has too much pride to ask for it, unfortunately.
b if he meets a determined opponent.
c when he has such an aggressive manner.
d it really isn't fair on him to have such a lot of responsibility.
e that leaves him so exhausted.
f it's no surprise he feels frustrated.

Exercise 3

Decide if the pairs of sentences have the same meaning.

1. **A** The project was rejected after all Boris's hard work, and he was so exhausted he thought about leaving the company.
   B The rejection of the project after all his hard work left Boris so frustrated he considered leaving the company. ☐

2. **A** I was absolutely horrified when I heard how you'd been treated by the officials.
   B I was totally shocked when I heard about the way the officials had treated you. ☐

3. **A** I think you should apologize for hurting Penny's feelings.
   B You ought to say sorry to Penny for upsetting her, in my opinion. ☐

4. **A** It's your own fault if you're miserable; you can't gossip about your friends and expect them not to be angry.
   B You've only got yourself to blame if you're lonely when you refuse to talk to people who try to be friendly. ☐

5. **A** My grandparents ought to have someone to clean the house but they're too proud to admit they need help since Granny broke her hip.
   B My grandparents need to find a cleaner because they're absolutely helpless since Granny broke her hip. ☐

Exercise 4

Choose the correct word.

A good teacher understands that young children's difficult behaviour may stem from a variety of causes, and not just the most obvious. Some children are naturally ¹**optimistic / sociable**, while others may come from families that are, for one reason or another, ²**suspicious / proud** of strangers, so the children are unused to everyday social interaction with new people and are ³**determined / puzzled** by overtures of friendship from their classmates.

Other children may want to make friends but fail because they lack the necessary skills, and in their ⁴**disgust / frustration** become ⁵**aggressive / guilty** towards the ones who have ⁶**upset / shocked** them.

It is up to the teacher to keep an eye on such children and help them to settle into the classroom.

Exercise 5

Are the highlighted words correct or incorrect in the sentences?

1. We must do something about the kitchen cupboards, they're in a **disgusting** ☐ state.
2. She has a very **fair** ☐ personality, always looking on the bright side.
3. Ian's behaviour frequently **upset** ☐ his colleagues and eventually he was asked to leave.
4. We will consider all the applications for the post and let the **determined** ☐ candidate know our decision by the end of the week.
5. Sandra was a popular girl, constantly being asked to parties, but her brother Mark was less **sociable** ☐ and rarely went with her.
6. Why are you always so **puzzled** ☐ when I offer to help you? Anyone would think you didn't trust me.

14

Music and the arts

Jan Hi, Diana. It's Jan. Did you have a good weekend?

Diana Yeah, it was great! We went to a really interesting **exhibition**. There were some quite **abstract** pieces of work. They really appealed to my imagination.

Jan Oh, really? I don't really like that kind of thing, to be honest. I went to a lovely concert, with this amazing **conductor** and **soloist**.

★★★★★

The last **track** on this album is by far the best. It has a **beat** that you can't resist tapping your foot along to, and **lyrics** that stay in your head for days. Each **verse** is a work of art in itself and the **chorus** is truly unforgettable…

Good to know!

It's often possible to add *-ist* to a musical instrument to make a word for the person who plays it — for example, *violinist*. A few words are different, though: for example, *drummer*.

Word Finder: arts

abstract	1 ADJECTIVE **Abstract** art makes use of shapes and patterns rather than showing people or things. 2 NOUN An **abstract** is an abstract work of art.
exhibit	NOUN An **exhibit** is a painting, sculpture or other object of interest that is displayed in a museum or art gallery.
exhibition	NOUN An **exhibition** is a public event at which pictures, sculptures, or other objects of interest are displayed, for example at a museum or art gallery.
landscape	NOUN A **landscape** is a painting that shows a scene in the countryside.
model	NOUN An artist's **model** is a person who stays still in a particular position so that the artist can make a picture or sculpture of them.
portrait	NOUN A **portrait** is a painting, drawing, or photograph of a particular person.

55

Word Finder: music

backing group	NOUN A **backing group** is a group of singers or musicians who accompany the main singer.
beat	NOUN The **beat** of a piece of music is the main rhythm that it has.
chorus	NOUN A **chorus** is a part of a song that is repeated after each verse.
conductor	NOUN A **conductor** is a person who stands in front of an orchestra or choir and directs its performance.
drum kit	NOUN A **drum kit** is a set of drums and cymbals.
gig	NOUN A **gig** is a live performance by someone such as a musician or a comedian.
lead guitarist	NOUN A **lead guitarist** is the main guitar player in a group or band.
bass guitarist	NOUN A **bass guitarist** is the guitar player who plays a guitar that produces a very deep sound.
lyrics	NOUN The **lyrics** of a song are its words.
melody	NOUN A **melody** is a tune.
read music	PHRASE If you can **read music**, you have the ability to look at and understand the symbols that are used in written music to represent musical sounds.
rhythm	NOUN A **rhythm** is a regular series of sounds or movements.
soloist	NOUN A **soloist** is a musician or dancer who performs a solo.
track	NOUN A **track** is one of the songs or pieces of music on a CD, record, or tape.
verse	NOUN A **verse** is one of the parts into which a poem or a song is divided.
vocalist	NOUN A **vocalist** is a singer who sings with a pop group.

Exercise 1

Put the correct word in each gap.

exhibition | melody | portrait | abstract | model | landscape

1 A type of painting that makes use of shapes and patterns rather than showing people or things: _____
2 A painting, drawing or photograph of a particular person: _____
3 A public event at which pictures, sculptures or other objects of interest are displayed, for example at a museum or art gallery: _____
4 A painting that shows a scene in the countryside: _____
5 A person who stays still, in a particular position, so that an artist can make a picture or sculpture of them: _____

Work on your Vocabulary Upper Intermediate (B2)

Exercise 2

Find the words or phrases that do not belong, as shown.

1 Connected with songs	lyrics	melody	model
2 Types of painting	landscape	gig	portrait
3 Regular patterns of sounds	melody	beat	rhythm
4 Parts of songs	track	chorus	verse
5 Individual musicians	lead guitarist	soloist	backing group
6 Events that people go to	gig	exhibition	portrait
7 People who sing	conductor	backing group	vocalist

Exercise 3

Choose the correct word.

1 You didn't tell me you could read **music / rhythm / melody**.
2 The **vocalist / chorus / track** is often repeated in a song. It's the most memorable part.
3 Would you like to go to a **gig / lyric / beat** the weekend after next?
4 I don't understand **portrait / landscape / abstract** art; I prefer paintings to represent real-life objects.
5 It must be difficult to be a **soloist / model / conductor**; I don't know how they can stand completely still for so long.

Exercise 4

Write the correct form of the word in brackets to complete each sentence.

1 At the end of the performance, the _____ (conduct) asked the orchestra to stand up and take a bow.
2 The _____ (solo) was very nervous; you could hear her voice shaking.
3 Imran isn't very good at playing the drums, because he has no sense of _____ (rhythmic) at all.
4 The bass _____ (guitar) in a band helps keep the beat of a song.
5 Songwriters often work in pairs. One person writes the ª_____ (melodic) and the other writes the ᵇ_____ (lyrical).
6 The lead vocalist's voice was quite weak, but his _____ (back) group were amazing, I think.

Exercise 5
Choose the correct word.

There's something for everyone at the Hadstock Arts Festival!

Monday: Jazz ¹**conductor / vocalist / guitarist** Alex West will be starting the festival in style, singing some new ²**tracks / verses / choruses** from his latest album.

Tuesday: Do you think you have hidden artistic talent? If so, why not try your hand at painting an acrylic ³**portrait / abstract / landscape** of your favourite countryside scene for our competition? The winning entry will be displayed at the Mumford Gallery summer ⁴**model / gig / exhibition**.

Wednesday: Come and make some noise at our drum workshop! You don't need a drum kit, but a good sense of ⁵**melody / rhythm / lyrics** will help you to keep the beat. Don't worry if you can't read ⁶**melody / verse / music**, as everything we play is simple and easy to learn.

Exercise 6
Put the correct word in each gap.

| conductor | guitarist | beat | kit | music | melody | soloist |

Cantamos describe themselves as 'a choir with a difference'. According to their website, none of the members can read ¹_____, with the exception of the choir's ²_____, Andrew Cocker, who writes the choir's songs and directs their performances. Tickets to last week's concert were expensive, so I was expecting great things. Thankfully, I wasn't disappointed. The songs all had a strong ³_____ which got my feet tapping to the rhythm. The quality of the vocalists was extremely high for an amateur choir, but special mention needs to be made of the ⁴_____ who sang an extremely difficult Spanish ⁵_____ perfectly. His voice was like that of a professional singer's. The only low point of the whole performance was the band. The lead ⁶_____ was so loud that I couldn't hear the choir at certain points. The deafening drum ⁷_____ should also be replaced with a quieter instrument. All in all though, it was a most enjoyable evening.

15 Crime and law

Read the news report of the trial of former rugby star Grant Potts.

Potts not guilty

In a surprise decision, the **jury** in the **trial** of former rugby star Grant Potts yesterday **found him not guilty** of causing death by dangerous driving. Potts was **arrested** shortly after the car accident which killed his girlfriend, Lorna Woods. Geoffrey Dewar, who is **defending** Potts, said that his client was devastated by the accident, but always maintained his **innocence**. 'It was simply a tragic accident', he said. Lorna Woods' father disagreed. 'This is not **justice**', he said outside the **court**. 'That man is a **criminal**. He killed my daughter and the **judge** has **let** him **off**.'

> **Good to know!**
>
> In British English, <u>jury</u> can be followed by a singular or a plural verb.
>
> The jury <u>has</u> to listen to all the evidence.
>
> The jury <u>were</u> asked to consider these facts.
>
> In American English, a singular verb must be used.

Word Finder

arrest	VERB If the police **arrest** someone, they take charge of them and take them to a police station, because they believe they may have committed a crime.
break the law	PHRASE If someone **breaks the law**, they do something that is not allowed by the law.
burglar	NOUN A **burglar** is someone who enters a building by force and steals things.
burglary	NOUN If someone commits a **burglary**, they enter a building by force and steal things.
charge	VERB When the police **charge** someone, they formally accuse them of having done something illegal.
commit a crime	PHRASE If someone **commits a crime**, they do something that is a crime.

	court	NOUN A **court** is a place where legal matters are decided by a judge and jury.
	criminal	NOUN A **criminal** is a person who regularly commits crimes.
	defend	VERB When a lawyer **defends** a person who has been accused of something, the lawyer argues on their behalf in a court of law that the charges are not true.
	find someone guilty / not guilty	PHRASE If a jury **finds someone guilty**, they decide that the person did commit the crime of which they are accused. If a jury **finds** the person **not guilty**, they decide that they did not commit the crime.
	illegal	ADJECTIVE If something is **illegal**, the law says that it is not allowed.
	illegally	ADVERB If something is done **illegally**, it is done in a way that is not allowed by law.
	innocence	NOUN If someone proves their **innocence**, they prove that they are not guilty of a crime.
	innocent	ADJECTIVE If someone is **innocent**, they have not committed a crime.
	innocently	ADVERB If something is done **innocently**, it is done by someone who does not intend to do anything wrong or to commit a crime.
	judge	NOUN A **judge** is the person in a court of law who decides how the law should be applied, for example how criminals should be punished.
	jury	NOUN In a court of law, the **jury** is the group of people who have been chosen from the general public to listen to the facts about a crime and to decide whether the person accused is guilty or not.
	justice	NOUN **Justice** is the legal system that a country uses in order to punish people who break the law.
	law	NOUN The **law** is a system of rules that a society or government develops in order to deal with crime, business agreements, and social relationships.
	legal	ADJECTIVE If something is **legal**, the law says that it is allowed.
	legally	ADVERB If something is done **legally**, it is done in a way that is allowed by law.
	let someone off	PHRASAL VERB To **let someone off** means not to punish them for a crime.
	punishment	NOUN A **punishment** is a particular way of punishing someone.
	trial	NOUN A **trial** is a formal meeting in a law court, at which a judge and jury listen to evidence and decide whether a person is guilty of a crime.
	witness	NOUN A **witness** to an event such as an accident or crime is a person who saw it.

UNIT 15 Crime and law

Exercise 1
Put the correct word or phrase in each gap.

| charged | judge | arrested | innocent | committed a crime | innocence | burglary | break the law | found guilty |

James Wilson was ¹_____ by police yesterday during a raid on his home in Sullivan Street and ²_____ with a series of offences, including ³_____. Wilson protested his ⁴_____, claiming he had never ⁵_____ in his life. He is due to appear before a ⁶_____ on 17 September.

Exercise 2
Choose the correct word.

Marian Bailey appeared in ¹**trial / court / jury** on Monday, ²**charged / defended / arrested** with causing criminal damage. She claimed to be ³**guilty / innocent / legal**, but three ⁴**witnesses / juries / burglars** provided evidence against her. In ⁵**deciding / saying / finding** her guilty, the ⁶**judge / lawyer / police** said he believed the maximum ⁷**justice / defence / punishment** allowed by law was inadequate in such a serious case.

Exercise 3
Rearrange the letters to find words. Use the definitions to help you.

1 stewsin _____ (a person who sees a crime being committed)
2 ryuj _____ (a group of people chosen to listen to the facts about a crime and decide whether the person accused is guilty or not)
3 tejiscu _____ (the system that a country uses in order to deal with people who break the law)
4 gyrrubal _____ (entering a building by force and stealing things)
5 liricman _____ (a person who has committed a crime)
6 deguj _____ (a person in a court who decides how the law should be applied)

Exercise 4
Complete the text by writing one word in each gap.

The homeowners reported that somebody had broken into their house and stolen some jewellery. Patrick Sullivan was arrested the next day and ¹_____ with burglary and the ²_____ sale of property. At his ³_____, both the homeowners and his own son appeared as ⁴_____ for the prosecution and he was ⁵_____ guilty. He was sentenced to two years' imprisonment and he left the court proclaiming his ⁶_____.

Exercise 5
Complete the sentences by writing a word or a phrase in each gap.

| break the law | criminal | let off | committed a crime |
| punishment | jury | law | defend |

1 The criminal expected to be sent to prison, but he was _____ with a fine.
2 The judge felt that as the accused had already suffered a great deal, she should receive a light _____.
3 The accused chose to _____ himself in court, as he believed he could present his case better than a lawyer.
4 The woman explained in detail the circumstances that had led her to _____.
5 Stephenson admitted that he had _____, but argued that nobody had suffered as a result.
6 After six hours of deliberations, the _____ was still unable to reach a verdict.

Exercise 6
Which sentences are correct?

1 My neighbour was arrested and defended with burglary. ❑
2 Although the judge clearly thought the woman had committed the crime, the jury found her not guilty. ❑
3 The court was packed for the trial and the accused defended themselves against all the charges. ❑
4 Lawyers, judges and juries are all part of the machinery of justice. ❑
5 One of the problems of arresting people to prison is that they can learn from other criminals. ❑
6 There was a public uproar when the men charged with murder were let off. ❑

16 Communication

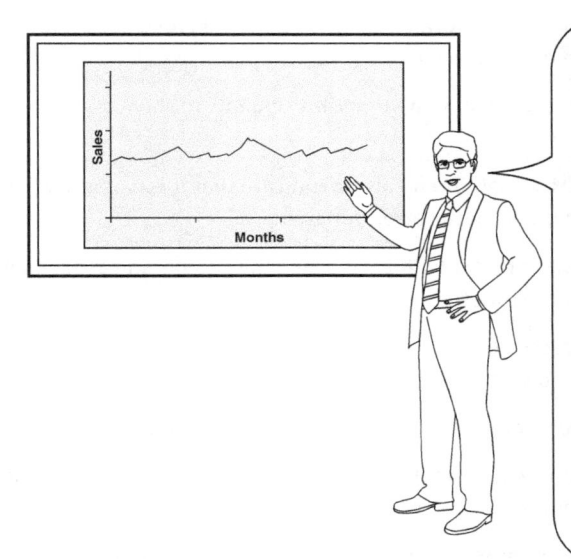

Good morning, everyone. I've called this meeting in order to **update** you on the company's performance over the last three months. As you can see from this **chart**, sales have been level. However, the figures are slightly **misleading**, because they do not include a huge deal to Brazil, for which we are due to receive payment next month.

I must **emphasize** that the current economic situation is not encouraging, and we must all work hard to **get across** the message that our products may not be the cheapest, but the quality is second to none!

So, to **sum up**, we are doing well at the moment, but we must continue to fight to stay ahead of the competition.

Last week I found Julie looking really upset. Apparently she and Jack had **quarrelled** about their college work. Julie felt that Jack was **boasting** about his grades. She was particularly hurt by the tone of what he said. She is finding the work difficult, and he seemed to be implying she was stupid.

I decided to **have a word with** Jack, and he was really shocked. He said he'd only meant to offer to help her, and he didn't realize he'd offended her. He phoned her later to **clear up** the misunderstanding, and now they're great friends again.

Word Finder

account	NOUN An **account** is a written or spoken report of something that has happened.
boast	VERB If someone **boasts** about something, they talk about it very proudly, in a way that other people may find irritating or offensive.
catch someone's attention	PHRASE If you **catch someone's attention**, you make them notice you.
chart	NOUN A **chart** is a diagram, picture, or graph that is intended to make information easier to understand.
clear something up	PHRASAL VERB If someone **clears up** a misunderstanding, they explain it and deal with it.
deliver a speech	PHRASE If someone **delivers a speech**, they give a formal talk to an audience.

	draft	NOUN A **draft** is an early version of a letter, book, or speech.
	emphasize	VERB To **emphasize** something means to indicate that it is particularly important or to draw special attention to it.
	fluency	NOUN **Fluency** in a language is the ability to speak it well.
	get something across	PHRASAL VERB If someone **gets** a message or a point **across**, they manage to make people understand it.
	have a word with someone	PHRASE If you **have a word with someone**, you talk to them about something.
	highlight	VERB To **highlight** something means to indicate that it is particularly important or to draw special attention to it.
	interact	VERB When people **interact** with each other, they communicate as they work or spend time together.
	misleading	ADJECTIVE If you describe something as **misleading**, you mean that it gives you a wrong idea or impression.
	quarrel	VERB When two or more people **quarrel**, they have an angry argument.
	smartphone	NOUN A **smartphone** is a mobile phone that has many of the capabilities of a small computer, and can be used to access the Internet.
	sum up	PHRASAL VERB If you **sum** something **up**, you describe or repeat it as briefly as possible.
	tone	NOUN The **tone** of a speech or piece of writing is its style and the opinions or ideas expressed in it.
	underline	VERB If you **underline** something, you draw attention to it and emphasize its importance.
	update	VERB If you **update** someone on a situation, you tell them the latest developments in that situation.

Exercise 1

Match the sentence halves.

1 The restaurant was very busy, so Tom
2 Sarah needed to speak to her boss urgently, so she
3 Jack's audience wasn't friendly, but he still managed to
4 Ben forgot his briefcase and had to
5 The misunderstanding over the contract was soon
6 At the end of his essay, Dan remembered to

a couldn't catch the waiters' attention.
b deliver his speech without notes.
c cleared up by management.
d had a word with him after the meeting.
e sum up his main points.
f get his message across.

UNIT 16 Communication

Exercise 2
Choose the correct word or phrase.
1 Jack underlined parts of the document to **update / interact / emphasize** their importance.
2 When Tim delivered his speech, his **fluency / words / talking** was impressive.
3 No one likes Graham – he's **quarrelled / interacted / boasted** with almost everyone in the office.
4 Our company has issued everyone with a **manual / smartphone / camera** so that the office can always contact them.
5 James gave us an interesting **talk / speech / account** of his recent business trip.
6 At the end of the meeting, the boss **summed up / made up / came up** his aims for next year.

Exercise 3
Rearrange the letters to find words. Use the definitions to help you.
1 ghihtilgh _____ (emphasize something important)
2 iialmsedgn _____ (encouraging belief in something that is not true, or not based on evidence)
3 pudtea _____ (give the latest information about something)
4 trahc _____ (a visual way of presenting information, e.g. figures)
5 frtad _____ (an early, unfinished version of, for example, a speech or a plan)
6 cratinte _____ (talk with other people)

Exercise 4
Complete the sentences by writing one word in each gap.

| clear | misleading | tone | boasts | charts | draft |

1 Simon asked his secretary to check the first _____ of his speech.
2 The lecturer showed us some very useful _____ during his presentation.
3 Tim always _____ about his achievements to anyone who'll listen.
4 I could tell from the _____ of Harry's voice that he was unhappy.
5 We'll have to _____ up a few points before we can reach an agreement.
6 Reviews of the film were very _____, so it wasn't really what we were expecting.

Exercise 5
Are the highlighted words correct or incorrect in the sentences?
1 It was a strange story in the newspaper that **brought** ❏ Bill's attention.
2 John was nervous about **delivering** ❏ a speech to such a big audience.
3 Simon wanted to **speak** ❏ a word with his teacher before the class.
4 Please go through this essay and **underline** ❏ the main points.
5 Jane needs to **update** ❏ some programs on her computer.
6 Stella's just had a big **quarrelling** ❏ with her sister.

17

Words and phrases for linking ideas

In this unit you learn some words and phrases that can help you link your ideas. These words and phrases are often called **discourse markers**.

Sasha I think you should do some of the housework, Ben. **After all**, you live here too.

Ben But I have so much studying to do. And **besides**, I pay more for my room than you do.

Sasha That's not a good reason! **In the first place**, you pay more because your room's bigger, and **in any case**, that has nothing to do with the housework.

Ben My parents are putting huge pressure on me to do well in my exams, and **at the same time** you're saying I should do more here. It's just too much!

Sasha I understand that your exams are important **of course**, but **even so**, I don't think it's fair to leave all the housework to us.

Dear Sir/Madam

With reference to your letter of January 16th, I am writing to tell you that you will not be receiving payment for your work until I am satisfied that modifications have been made **as follows**:

a) pipework in the kitchen area should be boxed in
b) damage from leaks should be repaired.

Furthermore, I would like to record my dissatisfaction with your staff. They were **not only** slow and inefficient, **but also** most impolite.

As a consequence of these experiences, I will not be recommending your company to anyone else. **What is more**, I am prepared to take this matter to court if it is not resolved promptly.

Yours

Mr H. Edwards

Mr H. Edwards

Words and phrases for linking ideas

after all	PHRASE	You use **after all** when introducing a statement that supports or helps explain something you have just said.
as a consequence	PHRASE	You use **as a consequence** when saying what happened as the result of something you have just talked about.
as follows	PHRASE	You use **as follows** to introduce something such as a list, description or explanation.
at any rate	PHRASE	You use **at any rate** to show that something is more important or more precise than what you have just said.
at the same time	PHRASE	You use **at the same time** to introduce something that is also true.
besides	ADVERB	**Besides** is used to emphasize an additional point that you are making.
even if / though	PHRASE	You use **even if** or **even though** to indicate that a particular fact does not make the rest of your statement untrue.
even so	PHRASE	You use **even so** to introduce a surprising fact that relates to what you have just said.
furthermore	ADVERB	**Furthermore** is used to introduce a piece of information or opinion that adds to or supports the previous one.
in any case	PHRASE	You say **in any case** after talking about things that you are not sure about, to emphasize that your next statement is the most important thing or the thing that you are sure about.
in other words	PHRASE	You say **in other words** to introduce a different, and usually simpler, explanation or interpretation of something that has just been said.
in the first place	PHRASE	You use **in the first place** to introduce the first in a series of points or reasons.
just as ... so	PHRASE	You use **just as ... so** to say that two things are similar.
nevertheless	ADVERB	You use **nevertheless** when saying something that contrasts with what has just been said.
not only ... but also	PHRASE	You use **not only ... but also** to emphasize that something is true, but that something else is true too.
of course	PHRASE	You use **of course** to show that there is a reason for something.
on the contrary	PHRASE	You use **on the contrary** when you have just said or implied that something is not true and are going to say that the opposite is true.
that is to say	PHRASE	You use **that is to say** to say something in a different way in order to explain it.
to conclude	PHRASE	You use **to conclude** to indicate that what you say next will be the last part of your speech or writing.
what is more	PHRASE	You use **what is more** to add another point to support your view about something.
with reference / regard / respect to	PHRASE	You use **with reference to**, **with regard to**, or **with respect to** in formal speech or writing to show what you are talking or writing about.

Exercise 1

Which sentences are correct?

1 It's worth considering the perspective of the interviewer if you're going for a job interview. After all, interviewers are human too. ❑
2 There was an explosion in the gas supply, and as follows, the whole house was destroyed. ❑
3 I was afraid of her, but at the same time, I was quite fond of her. ❑
4 He never dresses very smartly. Of course, he's not really interested in clothes. ❑
5 It looks like rain, but on the contrary, I'm going out for a walk. ❑
6 The concert was fully booked and in any case, most of us couldn't afford a ticket. ❑

Exercise 2

Choose the correct word or phrase.

1 I wouldn't go to his party **even if / what is more / even so** he begged me to go.
2 **Furthermore / In the first place / With reference to** your claim for compensation, we regret to inform you that the damage is not covered by your insurance policy.
3 Legal language is very difficult to understand. I don't understand it, **at any rate / on the contrary / at the same time**.
4 Cars pollute the environment, they're expensive and **besides / nevertheless / even so**, I've got nowhere to keep one.
5 **Not only / Just as / Even so** my parents married when they were in their teens, so did I.

Exercise 3

Are the highlighted words correct or incorrect in the sentences?

1 I'll meet you this afternoon. **That is to say** ❑, I will if I can leave work early.
2 They were refused admission to the club, **even so** ❑ they'd been there several times before.
3 You say Sandra is polite and friendly. **On the contrary** ❑, she's one of the rudest people I know.
4 So, ladies and gentlemen, **to conclude** ❑, I want us to look beyond our current problems and create a vision for the future.
5 Just as I value our heritage, **as** ❑ I understand the need for change.
6 My father-in-law is, **furthermore** ❑, a wholehearted supporter of our cause.

Exercise 4

Put the correct phrase in each gap.

| Even though | To conclude | Not only | As follows | On the contrary |
| In other words | In the first place | What is more |

I'd like to explain why I believe this company is facing a crisis. ¹_____, our losses have mounted in recent years and there is no sign of any improvement. ²_____ are costs rising, but we also face a decline in customer loyalty. ³_____, whereas ten or twenty years ago most of our customers would only buy our products, nowadays they buy whatever is on special offer. ⁴_____, competition in our market is fierce, and almost every month another new business enters the marketplace. ⁵_____ this company has been trading with considerable success for over a century, there is no guarantee that we will survive. ⁶_____, I would like to make a specific proposal for improving our position.

UNIT 17 Words and phrases for linking ideas

Exercise 5
Decide if the pairs of sentences have the same meaning.

1. **A** I am writing to you with regard to your letter of 17 April.
   B I was impressed by your letter of 17 April. ❑

2. **A** The police were not treated as enemies. On the contrary, they were welcomed as providing protection from criminals.
   B It is not true that the police were treated as enemies. The opposite is true: they were welcomed as providing protection from criminals. ❑

3. **A** Graham had warned her he might be late, after all, so she felt justified in starting dinner without him.
   B She felt justified in starting dinner without Graham because the last thing he had said was that he might be late. ❑

4. **A** The winners of the awards are as follows.
   B The winners of the awards are following me onto the platform. ❑

5. **A** He lost interest in farming, and as a consequence he started looking for an alternative source of employment.
   B The result of losing interest in farming was that he started looking for an alternative source of employment. ❑

Exercise 6
Write the missing word or phrase in sentence B so that it means the same as sentence A.

1. **A** I'll tell you the matters we need to discuss during the meeting.
   B The matters we need to discuss during the meeting are as _____.

2. **A** Cities are always crowded, noisy and dirty. Having said that, I couldn't imagine living anywhere else.
   B I couldn't imagine living anywhere else but a city, _____ they're always crowded, noisy and dirty.

3. **A** I think football is exciting both to play and to watch. Let me put it another way – it's the best sport in the world.
   B I think football is exciting both to play and to watch. _____, it's the best sport in the world.

4. **A** He may not be very sociable but I like him, although I'm not certain that other people do.
   B He may not be very sociable, but he's well-liked – by me, _____.

69

18

Work and jobs

Career Opportunities

Print Manager

PERFECT PRINTING LTD is seeking to **appoint** a new print manager in Norwich. This is a highly **skilled** position, requiring at least five years' experience. The ideal **candidate** will be efficient, energetic, and used to working to tight **deadlines**.

The company **supplies** printing services to different businesses throughout the region. The print manager will liaise with **clients** as well as overseeing the printing process. Some **shiftwork** may be required. The post comes with a competitive salary and generous **overtime** rates.

I was made **redundant** last year, and since then, things have been very difficult. Our household **income** is so low now that I struggle to **provide** everything for my family. I'm looking for a new job, but it's hard. There's so much **competition** for every job, and most of them don't offer **flexi-time**, which makes it difficult when you've got children to look after.

I've applied for a job at a care home. The **duties** include cleaning and cooking meals. I don't think it's a great place to work, though. The staff all went on **strike** last month because of the poor working conditions.

Word Finder

appoint	VERB If you **appoint** someone to a job or official position, you formally choose them for it.
candidate	NOUN A **candidate** is someone who is being considered for a job.
client	NOUN A **client** of a professional person or organization is a person or company that receives a service from them in return for payment.
commerce	NOUN **Commerce** is the activities and procedures involved in buying and selling things.
competition	NOUN **Competition** is an activity involving two or more firms, in which each firm tries to get people to buy its own goods in preference to the other firms' goods.
consultant	NOUN A **consultant** is a person who gives expert advice to a person or organization on a particular subject.

Work on your Vocabulary Upper Intermediate (B2)

UNIT 18 Work and jobs

crew	NOUN The **crew** of a ship, an aircraft, or a spacecraft is the group of people who work on and operate it.
deadline	NOUN A **deadline** is a time or date before which a particular task must be finished or a particular thing must be done.
deal	NOUN If you make a **deal**, you complete an agreement or an arrangement with someone, especially in business.
duty	NOUN Your **duties** are tasks that you have to do because they are part of your job.
establish	VERB If someone **establishes** something such as an organization or a business, they start it.
flexi-time	NOUN **Flexi-time** is a system that allows employees to vary the time that they start and finish work, provided that a particular total number of hours are spent at work.
income	NOUN A person's or organization's **income** is the money that they earn or receive, as opposed to the money that they have to spend or pay out.
overtime	NOUN **Overtime** is time that you spend doing your job in addition to your normal working hours.
provide	VERB If you **provide** something that someone needs or wants, or if you provide them with it, you give it to them or make it available to them.
redundant	ADJECTIVE If you are made **redundant**, your employer tells you to leave because your job is no longer necessary or because your employer cannot afford to keep paying you.
shiftwork	NOUN **Shiftwork** is a system where people such as nurses and factory workers work for a set period and are then replaced by people working for another period.
skilled	ADJECTIVE **Skilled** work can only be done by people who have had some training.
strike	NOUN When there is a **strike**, workers stop doing their work for a period of time, usually in order to try to get better pay or conditions for themselves.
supply	VERB If you **supply** someone with something that they want or need, you give them a quantity of it.

Exercise 1

Choose the correct word.

1 These workers are on very low **spendings / incomes / payments**.
2 I think he would be a very good **candidate / client / dealer** for the job.
3 We are planning to **apply / establish / appoint** a new sales manager.
4 We are hoping to develop all areas of industry and **overtime / companies / commerce** in our nation.
5 This company employs a highly **redundant / skilled / responsible** workforce.
6 My employer allows me to work **flexi-time / shiftwork / deadlines** to fit my work around my studies.

Exercise 2

Put the correct word in each gap.

| duties | incomes | overtime | strike | consultant | provide |

An unhappy worker

I currently work in a large hotel, but I don't know how much longer I can stand my job. Six months ago, the managers brought in a ¹_____ to advise them on making cost savings. Since then, my ²_____ have increased so much that I can barely manage my work – in fact, I usually end up doing several hours of unpaid ³_____ every week.

The hotel doesn't even ⁴_____ our uniforms anymore. We have to buy them ourselves, even though most of us are on pretty low ⁵_____. Things have got so bad that we're seriously considering going on ⁶_____ for better pay and conditions.

Exercise 3

Which sentences are correct?

1 We are pleased to announce that Robert Watkins has been appointed as our new chief executive. ☐
2 Everyone had to make overtime in order to complete the work on time. ☐
3 Our products are cheaper and of higher quality than those produced by the competitions. ☐
4 Most of our editorial staff are allowed to work flexi-time. ☐
5 After two days of discussions, we reached a deal with our paper suppliers. ☐
6 The railway workers are planning to go to strike. ☐

Exercise 4

Match the sentence halves.

1 Luckily, we managed to do a deal on
2 My wife does shift work so
3 If I miss this deadline,
4 There are complex laws
5 Most of the crew
6 I have recently been asked

a a large order of wood.
b my boss will be very angry.
c to take on some additional duties.
d will join the ship in Piraeus.
e we're rarely at home together.
f to regulate international commerce.

72 *Work on your Vocabulary* Upper Intermediate (B2)

19 Travel and holidays

I had a meeting in London yesterday, and I decided to drive because I had a lot of stuff to take with me. What a disaster! It was **rush hour** of course, so the whole city turned into one big **traffic jam**, with everyone getting angry and sounding their **horns** at any opportunity. Actually, though, it was worse when the traffic got moving, with cars **pulling out** in front of me, changing **lanes** without signalling and trying to **overtake** when there really wasn't room. It was really scary, and to make it worse, I **turned up** at my meeting an hour late!

Trip itinerary

- Monday: 9 a.m. meet at **Terminal** 5, Heathrow airport. We will board the **aircraft** at around 11.30 a.m.. **Land** in New York early afternoon US time for 2-day **stopover**.
- Wednesday: **Scheduled** flight to Lima.
- Thursday and Friday: **Trekking** in the Andes.
- Saturday: Optional **parachute** jump.

Good to know!

It is important to note the pronunciation of <u>transport</u>. The noun has the stress on the first syllable (<u>trans</u>port). The verb has the stress on the second syllable (trans<u>port</u>).

Word Finder

aircraft	NOUN An **aircraft** is a vehicle which can fly, for example an aeroplane or a helicopter.
connection	NOUN If you get a **connection** at a station or airport, you catch a train, bus, or plane, after getting off another train, bus, or plane, in order to continue your journey.
deck	NOUN A **deck** on a vehicle such as a bus or ship is a lower or upper area of it.
get away	PHRASAL VERB If you **get away**, you go somewhere, often for a holiday.
horn	NOUN On a vehicle such as a car, the **horn** is the device that makes a loud noise as a signal or warning.
immigration	NOUN **Immigration** is the movement of people into a country in order to live and work there.

land	VERB	If an aircraft **lands**, or if someone in an aircraft **lands**, the aircraft comes down to the ground at the end of a journey.
lane	NOUN	A **lane** is a part of a main road that is marked by the edge of the road and a painted line, or by two painted lines.
overtake	VERB	If you **overtake** a vehicle or a person that is ahead of you and moving in the same direction, you pass them.
parachute	NOUN	A **parachute** is a device that enables a person to jump from an aircraft and float safely to the ground. It consists of a large piece of thin cloth attached to your body by strings.
pull out	PHRASAL VERB	If you **pull out**, you move your vehicle onto the road or onto a part of the road that is further out from the edge.
pull over	PHRASAL VERB	If you **pull over**, you move your car to the side of the road and stop.
pull up	PHRASAL VERB	If you **pull up**, you slow down and stop your car.
row	VERB	When you **row**, you sit in a boat and make it move through the water by using oars.
rush hour	NOUN	The **rush hour** is one of the periods of the day when most people are travelling to or from work.
scheduled	ADJECTIVE	A **scheduled** flight is a flight that goes at regular times.
stopover	NOUN	A **stopover** is a short stay in a place in between parts of a journey.
terminal	NOUN	A **terminal** is a place where vehicles, passengers, or goods begin or end a journey.
traffic jam	NOUN	A **traffic jam** is when there are so many vehicles on a road that they cannot move.
transport	1 NOUN	**Transport** refers to any vehicle that you can travel in or carry goods in.
	2 VERB	To **transport** people or goods somewhere is to take them from one place to another in a vehicle.
trekking	NOUN	If you go **trekking**, you go on a journey across difficult country, usually on foot.
turn up	PHRASAL VERB	If you **turn up** somewhere, you arrive there, often unexpectedly.

Exercise 1

Match the sentence halves.

1 The man was trying to overtake
2 I immediately sounded
3 She managed to land
4 We usually leave early to avoid
5 You need to get into
6 The train was late and the family missed

a their connection.
b a large lorry.
c the horn in order to warn them.
d the right-hand lane here.
e the aircraft in a field.
f the rush hour.

UNIT 19 Travel and holidays

Exercise 2

Put the correct word or phrase in each gap.

| landed | scheduled | immigration | stopover | terminal | get away |

Hi Bill

Just back from two weeks in the US. I decided I needed to ¹_____ for a bit, so I went to visit my old friend, Julia, in San Francisco. I managed to get a ²_____ flight from London for a reasonable price and it was such a great trip! The first thing was the fantastic view of the city and the ocean as we ³_____. It took ages to get through ⁴_____, but Julia was waiting for me in the ⁵_____ and it was wonderful to see her again. We had such a great time together and I had a three-day ⁶_____ in New York on the way back. Hope to meet up with you soon!

Love

Debbie

Exercise 3

Choose the correct word or phrase.

1 A huge lorry suddenly **pulled over / pulled out / turned out** in front of me, and I nearly crashed into it.
2 I felt seasick so I decided to **go on / go to / go up the** deck to get some fresh air.
3 She realized she was lost, so she **pulled over / pulled out / drove over** to look at the map.
4 When they get to Heathrow airport, they have a **link / change / connection** to Edinburgh.
5 We were late, because we were **held / stuck / kept** in a traffic jam.
6 What time did Shona **pull up / turn up / turn out** at the party?

Exercise 4

Put the correct word or phrase in each gap.

| your connection | goods | lanes | transport | a boat | flight |

1 change _____
2 miss _____
3 a scheduled _____
4 transport _____
5 row _____
6 public _____

Exercise 5

Complete the sentences by writing one word in each gap.

| aircraft | immigration | trekking | parachute | connection | terminal |

1 My cousin was killed when her _____ failed to open.
2 The _____ is equipped with a modern flight management system.
3 We plan to go _____ in Nepal.
4 Transport chiefs hope to build a new _____ at the airport.
5 The country has extremely strict _____ controls.
6 You should have time to make your _____ in Berlin.

Exercise 6

Are the highlighted words correct or incorrect in the sentences?

1 We pulled **up** ❏ outside the hotel.
2 We were unable to overtake **past** ❏ the tractor.
3 Make sure you get **onto** ❏ the right lane at the roundabout.
4 He turned **up** ❏ in Paris with no money and nowhere to live.
5 I want to get **off** ❏ with my family for a few days.
6 What is the best **form** ❏ of transport in this region?

Prefixes and suffixes

Prefixes are added to the beginning of words and suffixes to the end of words to form new words in the same family.

Prefixes

You will learn to use the following common prefixes in this unit:

Prefix	Meaning	Example
co-	with *or* together	**co**operative
dis-	not *or* the opposite of	**dis**honest, **dis**organized
il-, im-, ir-	not	**il**legal, **im**polite, **ir**regular
over-	too much *or* more than	**over**time
un-	not	**un**bearable, **un**fashionable
well-	well	**well**-organized

Suffixes

You will learn to use the following common suffixes in this unit:

Suffix	Meaning	Example
-able	able to be	unbearable
-al	relating to	functional
-ful	having that quality	faithful
-ic	having that quality	energetic, sympathetic
-ing	making someone feel a particular thing	misleading
-ive	having that quality or effect	offensive
-less	without	harmless
-like	similar to	lifelike
-ness	having that quality	loneliness
-proof	protecting against *or* not damaged by	waterproof

Common prefixes and suffixes

cooperative	ADJECTIVE A **cooperative** activity is done by people working together.
dishonest	ADJECTIVE If you say that a person or their behaviour is **dishonest**, you mean that they are not truthful or honest and that you cannot trust them.
disorganized	ADJECTIVE Something that is **disorganized** is in a confused state or is badly planned or organized.
energetic	ADJECTIVE An **energetic** person has a lot of energy and is very active.
faithful	ADJECTIVE If a person or animal is **faithful** to someone, they are loyal to that person.
functional	ADJECTIVE **Functional** equipment works or operates in the way that it is supposed to.
harmless	ADJECTIVE Something that is **harmless** does not have any bad effects, especially on people's health.
illegal	ADJECTIVE If something is **illegal**, the law says that it is not allowed.
impolite	ADJECTIVE If you say that someone is **impolite**, you mean that they are rather rude and do not have good manners.
irregular	ADJECTIVE Something that is **irregular** is not smooth or straight, or does not form a regular pattern.
lifelike	ADJECTIVE Something that is **lifelike** has the appearance of being alive.
loneliness	NOUN **Loneliness** is unhappiness that is felt by someone because they do not have any friends or do not have anyone to talk to.
misleading	ADJECTIVE If you describe something as **misleading**, you mean that it gives you a wrong idea or impression.
offensive	ADJECTIVE Something that is **offensive** upsets or embarrasses people because it is rude or insulting.
overtime	NOUN **Overtime** is time that you spend doing your job in addition to your normal working hours.
sympathetic	ADJECTIVE If you are **sympathetic** to someone who is in a bad situation, you are kind to them and show sympathy for their feelings.
unbearable	ADJECTIVE If you describe something as **unbearable**, you mean that it is so unpleasant, painful, or upsetting that you feel unable to accept it or deal with it.
unfashionable	ADJECTIVE If something is **unfashionable**, it is not modern, or is not liked or done by most people.
waterproof	ADJECTIVE Something that is **waterproof** does not let water pass through it.
well-organized	ADJECTIVE Something that is **well-organized** has been planned very carefully.

UNIT 20 Prefixes and suffixes

Exercise 1
Write the correct form of the word in brackets to complete each sentence.
1 It would be _____ (honest) to ignore the research findings, even though they aren't what we were hoping for.
2 My granddaughter is so _____ (energy) that I'm exhausted after I've spent an hour with her!
3 The other people on the bus found Ralph's behaviour so _____ (offend) that someone called the police.
4 The pain was so _____ (bear), Gillian had to ask her doctor for stronger painkillers.
5 Mona was worried when her child was stung by an insect, and was very relieved when it turned out to be _____ (harm).
6 The information Billy had been given proved to be _____ (lead), and he had to start the application process all over again.

Exercise 2
Choose the correct word.
1 Stop worrying about that spider. It's **harmless / misleading / huge** and won't hurt you.
2 My secretary is so **functional / cooperative / unfashionable**, she is always happy to help out when we get busy in the office.
3 Dogs are supposed to be **calm / energetic / faithful** creatures and will never leave their owners, but cats can just wander off.
4 Did you know that dropping litter is **illegal / dishonest / impossible** in some countries and you can be fined for it?
5 **Companionship / Loneliness / Privacy** is a terrible thing and many old people who have lost friends and family suffer from it.

Exercise 3
For each question, tick the correct answer.

1 Someone who is sympathetic
  ❏ cares about how other people are feeling.
  ❏ wants sympathy from other people.
  ❏ is worried about what other people think about them.

2 Someone who works overtime
  ❏ does shiftwork.
  ❏ is a temporary member of staff.
  ❏ works extra hours in their job.

3 If a gadget is functional, then it is
  ❏ complex.
  ❏ useful every day.
  ❏ difficult to use.

4 Waterproof fabric is often used to make
  ❏ underwear.
  ❏ raincoats.
  ❏ tablecloths.

5 A sculpture is lifelike if
  ❏ it is expensive to buy.
  ❏ it is made up of everyday materials.
  ❏ it looks like the real model.

Exercise 4

Match the two parts.

1 If someone is impolite,
2 If someone is unfashionable,
3 If someone is unbearable,
4 If someone is well-organized,
5 If someone's behaviour is irregular,
6 If someone is being misleading,

a no one wants to spend time with them.
b they are not acting as you would expect.
c they are not telling you the whole truth.
d they put all their things in the right place.
e they are rude to people.
f they often don't wear the latest fashions.

Exercise 5

Complete the sentences by writing one word in each gap.

1 Garry behaved really badly at the party last night. He hurt everyone's feelings by being _____ and aggressive.
2 Don't ask Alison if she has a copy of the notes from yesterday. She is so _____, she won't be able to find anything in her schoolbag.
3 This plastic fruit looks so _____, I could almost eat it.
4 Martin won't be able to join us tonight. He is still in the office doing _____, as usual.
5 These gloves are great. They are warm and _____ and don't even get wet when I make snowballs.
6 This email is very _____. Banks never ask for your password or ID like this. You should contact your bank and check it out.

Exercise 6

Rearrange the letters to find words. Use the definitions to help you.

1 lhramsse _____ (something that won't hurt you or cause you pain)
2 kllefiie _____ (a piece of art that looks very real)
3 vooaptrceie _____ (describing someone who will agree to do whatever you ask them to)
4 slslnenoie _____ (the feeling of being friendless and solitary)
5 gmnsldiiae _____ (making someone believe something that is not true)
6 ttmayicsphe _____ (someone who cares about the feelings of other people)

21

Register – formal vs. informal

Some words are only used in formal situations and some only in informal situations. It is important to know when a word is restricted like this so that you use it appropriately. A good dictionary will give you information about this.

Formal language

Words such as those in the following text are usually used only in formal situations and usually only in writing.

> Training sessions will **commence** at 9 a.m. next Monday. Please **ensure** that you have all necessary equipment with you. All recruits will be expected to **demonstrate** a high degree of maturity and willingness to learn. Any **persons** failing to comply with these rules will be removed from the session, and may **subsequently** be asked to leave the course.

Informal language

Words such as those in the following text are usually used only in informal situations, for example between friends. They are common in speech and informal writing such as text messages or emails.

> Did I tell you we've got a new **place** now? The rent's fifty **quid** a month more, but the big **plus** is that it has 3 bedrooms, so the **kids** can have a room each. My mum bought both of them a **telly** to have in their rooms, so they're really happy! The **guy** that owns the house is working abroad for two years, and his **mate** looks after it for him, and deals with the rent.

Formal and informal words

advantage / plus (*informal*)	NOUN	An **advantage** is a way in which one thing is better than another.
celebrity / celeb (*informal*)	NOUN	A **celebrity** is someone who is famous, especially in areas of entertainment such as films, music, writing, or sport.
commence (*formal*) / **begin, start**	VERB	When something **commences** or you **commence** it, it begins.
consequently (*formal*) / **so**	ADVERB	**Consequently** means as a result.
contradict (*formal*) / **go against**	VERB	If one policy, situation or statement **contradicts** another, there is a conflict between them, and they cannot both exist, be successful or be true.

Word Finder

demonstrate (*formal*) / **show**	VERB If you **demonstrate** a particular skill, quality, or feeling, you show by your actions that you have it.
ensure (*formal*) / **make sure**	VERB To **ensure** something, or to **ensure** that something happens, means to make certain that it happens.
friend / **mate, pal, buddy** (*informal*)	NOUN A **friend** is someone who you know well and like, but who is not related to you.
man / **bloke, guy** (*informal*)	NOUN A **man** is an adult male human being.
manager / **boss** (*informal*)	NOUN A **manager** is a person who is responsible for running part of or the whole of a business organization.
offspring, issue (*formal*) / **kids** (*informal*)	NOUN You can refer to a person's children as their **offspring**.
persons (*formal*) / **people**	NOUN **Persons** is a formal plural of the word 'person'.
police officer, policeman, policewoman / **cop** (*informal*)	NOUN A **police officer** is a member of the police force.
pound / **quid** (*informal*)	NOUN The **pound** is the unit of money that is used in the UK.
reside (*formal*) / **live**	VERB If someone **resides** somewhere, they live there or are staying there.
residence (*formal*) / **home** / **place** (*informal*)	NOUN A **residence** is a house where people live.
subsequently (*formal*) / **later, afterwards, then**	ADVERB **Subsequently** is used to introduce something that happened after the thing you have just mentioned.
sunglasses / **shades** (*informal*)	NOUN **Sunglasses** are glasses with dark lenses which you wear to protect your eyes from bright sunlight.
television / **telly, the box** (*informal*)	NOUN A **television** is a piece of electrical equipment consisting of a box with a glass screen on it on which you can watch programmes with pictures and sounds.
umbrella / **brolly** (*informal*)	NOUN An **umbrella** is an object that you use to protect yourself from the rain or hot sun. It consists of a long stick with a folding frame covered in cloth.

Exercise 1

Complete the sentences by writing one word in each gap.

| persons | commencing | offspring | residing | ensuring | residence |

1 The sign read 'No _____ under 21 admitted'.
2 According to this form, 'The allowance will no longer be paid to persons who are _____ abroad'.
3 A 30% deposit is to be paid prior to work _____.
4 Nearly all birds provide extended care for their _____.
5 The first term of the course is largely devoted to _____ that all students possess adequate background knowledge of the subject.
6 The White House is the official _____ of the President of the United States.

UNIT 21 Register – formal vs. informal

Exercise 2

Match the two parts.

1 umbrella
2 television
3 sunglasses
4 pound
5 manager
6 friend
7 offspring
8 advantage

a the box
b plus
c boss
d brolly
e quid
f mate
g shades
h kids

Exercise 3

Put the correct word or words in each gap.

| bloke | the box | buddies | shades | plus | quid |

Hey mate

Good to see you last night. It's a cool bar, isn't it? (And a real ¹_____ that it's five minutes from my front door!) Really nice to meet your ²_____ too. Tom seems like a great ³_____. I didn't leave my ⁴_____ at your place last night, did I? (Quite annoying not to have them today, as it was so sunny.) I hope I haven't lost them, as they cost me 50 ⁵_____!

Don't know about you, but I'm chilling tonight. Will probably spend most of it in front of ⁶_____ watching the footie.

Cheers!

Phil

Exercise 4

For each question, tick the correct answer.

1 What is a less formal way of saying 'subsequently'?
   ❏ for this reason
   ❏ afterwards
   ❏ sadly

2 What is an informal word for 'police officer'?
   ❏ cop
   ❏ pal
   ❏ mate

3 What is an informal word for 'umbrella'?
   ❏ telly
   ❏ brolly
   ❏ cuppa

4 What is a less formal way of saying 'commence'?
   ❏ decrease
   ❏ end
   ❏ start

5 What is an informal word for 'sunglasses'?
   ❏ shades
   ❏ biccies
   ❏ choccies

6 What is a less formal way of saying 'offspring'?
   ❏ fans
   ❏ children
   ❏ problems

22 Words that are used together (collocations)

A collocation is two or more words that are often used together. You need to learn collocations in order to use English in a natural way. For instance, we say that someone **commits a crime**. It does not sound natural to say ~~do a crime~~. It is often not possible to guess what collocations to use, so you need to learn them or look in a good dictionary. Look at the way collocations are used in this dialogue:

> **Patsy** I'm going to **come** straight **to the point**, Maria. I don't think you should marry Matt.
>
> **Maria** But why not? He's promised me that when he gets out of prison he's going to make a **fresh start**. He wants to settle down and **raise a family** of his own.
>
> **Patsy** Maria, you know that he never **keeps** his **promises**. He doesn't have any qualifications or any skills – how's he going to **make a living**? It's always the same. He says he's going to change. He says he wants a steady job with a **steady income**, but it never works out, and then he **commits** another **crime**.
>
> **Maria** But this time his uncle has offered him a job. He'll be able to **gain** some **experience** in his uncle's firm. I do know I'll be **taking a chance** if I marry him, but I really think he'll change this time.

Common collocations

catch fire	PHRASE	If something **catches fire**, it starts to burn.
catch someone's eye	PHRASE	If something **catches** your **eye**, you notice it.
catch sight of	PHRASE	If you **catch sight of** something, you see it briefly.
change the subject	PHRASE	If you **change the subject**, you start talking about something else.
come second	PHRASE	If a person or team **comes second**, they do not win but they get the next place.
come to the point	PHRASE	If someone **comes to the point**, they say the thing they intended to say.
commit a crime	PHRASE	If someone **commits a crime**, they do something that is a crime.
fresh start	PHRASE	If someone makes a **fresh start**, they begin something again.
gain experience	PHRASE	If someone **gains experience**, they get more knowledge or skill in a particular job or activity.
give a presentation	PHRASE	When someone **gives a presentation**, they give a formal talk.
heavy traffic	PHRASE	If there is **heavy traffic**, there are a lot of vehicles on a road.
keep a promise	PHRASE	If someone **keeps their promise**, they do what they promised to do.
keep calm	PHRASE	If someone **keeps calm**, they do not panic or become angry.

UNIT 22 Words that are used together (collocations)

make a living	PHRASE If someone **makes a living** in a particular way, that is how they earn money to live.
make a profit	PHRASE If a person or organization **makes a profit**, they end up with more money than they started with.
meet a deadline	PHRASE If someone **meets a deadline**, they do a task by the time it was supposed to be done.
raise a family	PHRASE Someone who **raises a family** looks after them until they are grown up.
steady income	PHRASE If you have a **steady income**, you get money regularly.
take a chance	PHRASE If you **take a chance**, you do something that has risks.
tell the difference	PHRASE If you can **tell the difference** between things, you can see that they are different.

Exercise 1

Match the sentence halves.

1 Guy dropped a burning match onto the grass and it
2 Gideon had a huge number of assignments, so he was struggling to
3 Daria was looking for a job with regular hours, because she wanted
4 In Morgan's former job, he often
5 Esther and Adam got married, settled down and
6 Sam and Tom were twins who looked so alike that most people couldn't

a tell the difference between them.
b gave presentations to other managers.
c to have a steady income.
d instantly caught fire.
e raised a family.
f meet all his deadlines.

Exercise 2

Choose the correct word.

1 If you make a promise to someone, you have to **do / keep / hold** it.
2 Artists can't always sell enough of their work and may even struggle to **get / find / make** a living.
3 Adrian was walking past a department store window when a fantastic bargain **caught / got / looked** his eye.
4 Leora was obviously embarrassed by what her husband was saying, so he quickly **broke / moved / changed** the subject.
5 We were late getting to the children's hospital, because the traffic was so **big / heavy / strong**.
6 Amil wasn't convinced his innovative idea would work, but he decided to **take / make / catch** a chance.

85

Exercise 3
Complete the sentences by writing one word in each gap.

| crime | sight | experience | point | start | second |

1 We lost our friend Ryan in the crowd, but then I caught _____ of him in the distance.
2 Ali was disappointed to come _____ when he'd expected to win the race.
3 The lecturer was fairly boring. It took ages for him to come to the _____.
4 If you commit a _____, you can expect to be punished by the state.
5 Yasmin's parents decided to make a fresh _____ and move from the city to the countryside.
6 Carlo asked the company if he could work there without pay, in order to gain some _____.

Exercise 4
Choose the correct word.

Hi Max

How are you? Daniel and I are finally beginning to ¹**make / do / raise** a profit in our new business and bring in a ²**steady / straight / steep** income. So it's very exciting, but we're trying to ³**go / set / keep** calm and continue to ⁴**gain / meet / hold** all our deadlines. I'm due to ⁵**tell / give / bring** a presentation tomorrow at the Bridge Hotel about the business. So let's hope it goes well. Anyway, now to ⁶**make / set / change** the subject completely – we're having a family barbecue on Saturday, so please do come!

Exercise 5
Put each sentence into the correct order.

1 of / caught / I / sight / in / Amir / crowd / the /.
_____

2 majestic / That / tree / fire / caught / old / has /.
_____

3 tell / can't / I / the / between / difference / wines / these /.
_____

4 hardly / Jack / living / a / work / makes / his / from /.
_____

5 traffic / so / The / we / was / heavy / late / were / that /.
_____

6 wants / Hannah / raise / countryside / to / her / the / in / family /.
_____

86 **Work on your Vocabulary** Upper Intermediate (B2)

23 Education

PHILOSOPHY SUMMER SCHOOL

Come and join our highly respected philosophy summer school! Staying on the lovely university **campus**, you will be able to concentrate on your studies without distraction. All our **tutors** are highly qualified, and the course includes both lectures and **workshops**, where students have the chance to develop work of their own.

The first week is general, and after that, students will have the chance to **specialize** in areas of particular interest. Each student will have a one-to-one **tutorial** every week.

Students do not have to **sit an exam**, but will be expected to complete two **assignments** over the three-week course. Successful students will be awarded a **certificate** at the end of the course.

For more information, go to www.summer-school.truro.ac.uk

I never imagined that I would go into **further education** because I wasn't very **academic** at school. However, when I was in my twenties I started doing evening classes in archaeology, and I enjoyed them so much that I decided to study for a degree. I was working at the time, so I did a part-time course, earning **credits** each year. I wrote my **dissertation** on the Minoan sites in Crete. I eventually **graduated** last year, and am now looking for a job connected with archaeology **research**.

Word Finder

	academic	1 ADJECTIVE **Academic** is used to describe things that relate to the work done in schools, colleges, and universities, especially work which involves studying and reasoning rather than practical or technical skills.
		2 ADJECTIVE Someone who is **academic** is good at studying.
	admission	NOUN **Admission** to a place such as a university is permission to enter it.
	assignment	NOUN An **assignment** is a task or piece of work that you are given to do, especially as part of your job or studies.
	campus	NOUN A **campus** is an area of land that contains the main buildings of a university or college.
	certificate	NOUN A **certificate** is an official document that you receive when you have completed a course of study or training.

credit		NOUN A **credit** is a successfully completed part of a higher education course.
debate		1 NOUN A **debate** is a discussion about a subject on which people have different views.
		2 VERB If people **debate** a topic, they discuss it formally, putting forward different views.
dissertation		NOUN A **dissertation** is a long formal piece of writing on a particular subject, especially for a university degree.
do / sit / take an exam		PHRASE If you **do an exam**, **sit an exam**, or **take an exam**, you do a formal test to show your knowledge or ability in a particular subject.
further education		NOUN **Further education** is the education that people do after they have left school.
graduate		1 NOUN In Britain, a **graduate** is a person who has successfully completed a degree at a university or college and has received a certificate that shows this.
		2 VERB In Britain, when a student **graduates** from university, they have successfully completed a degree course.
qualify		VERB When someone **qualifies**, they pass the examinations that they need to be able to work in a particular profession.
research		1 NOUN **Research** is work that involves studying something and trying to discover facts about it.
		2 VERB If you **research** something, you try to discover facts about it.
seminar		NOUN A **seminar** is a meeting where a group of people discuss a problem or topic.
slide		NOUN A **slide** is a picture that you show on a screen as part of a presentation or lecture.
specialize		VERB If you **specialize** in a particular subject, you study it and know a lot about it.
thesis		NOUN A **thesis** is a long piece of writing based on your own ideas and research that you do as part of a university degree, especially a higher degree such as a PhD.
tutor		NOUN A **tutor** is a teacher at a British university or college. In some American universities or colleges, a tutor is a teacher of the lowest rank.
tutorial		NOUN In a university or college, a **tutorial** is a regular meeting between a tutor and one or several students, for discussion of a subject that is being studied.
workshop		NOUN A **workshop** is a period of discussion or practical work on a particular subject in which a group of people share their knowledge or experience.

UNIT 23 Education

Exercise 1
Match the two parts.

1 The area of land containing the main buildings of a college or university is called
2 A long piece of writing based on your own ideas and research that you do as part of a university degree is called
3 A period of discussion or practical work on a particular subject in which a group of people share their knowledge or experience is called
4 A regular meeting between a university lecturer and one or several students to discuss a subject that is being studied is called
5 When you are allowed to join a university or college, you are granted
6 Someone who has finished their university course and been awarded a degree is called

a a workshop.
b a tutorial.
c a graduate.
d admission.
e the campus.
f a thesis.

Exercise 2
Rearrange the letters to find words. Use the definitions to help you.

1 ecrdti _____ (a successfully completed part of a higher education course)
2 nraimse _____ (a meeting where a group of people discuss a problem or topic)
3 desil _____ (a small piece of photographic film or a page in an electronic file that you project onto a large screen so that those present can see it)
4 uargetda _____ (a person who has successfully completed a degree at a university or college)
5 fitcreietac _____ (an official document that you receive when you have completed a course of study or training)
6 tehrfru duetcaino _____ (formal education after leaving school which does not take place at a university)

Exercise 3
Find the words that do not belong, as shown.

1 **Learning sessions**
   workshop   (certificate)   seminar   (slide)
2 **Pieces of written work**
   campus   dissertation   tutorial   assignment
3 **Words that can function as both verbs and nouns**
   specialize   debate   graduate   admission
4 **People**
   graduates   tutors   theses   credits

89

Exercise 4
Put the correct word in each gap.

dissertation | workshop | certificate | graduate | seminar | assignment | tutor

1 written coursework _____ _____
2 events _____ _____
3 people _____ _____

Exercise 5
Which sentences are correct?

1 When are you going to graduate? ❏
2 For your next assignment, you will need to make some research. ❏
3 We discussed the causes of three different wars during our tutor. ❏
4 Donna has just qualified as a vet. ❏
5 Silence please! Students are passing their exam in the hall. ❏
6 Raoul has always been very academic so he should do well at university. ❏

Exercise 6
Complete the sentences by writing one word in each gap.

admission | slides | tutorial | thesis | debates | qualifies | specializes | academic

1 What should we put on the first and last _____ in our presentation?
2 My _____ is at 9.30 a.m. on Thursday.
3 I've got to hand in my 60-page _____ next week.
4 Jessie has just gained _____ to the university that is her top choice.
5 Mr Hill lectures in philosophy and _____ in medical ethics.
6 This course _____ you to work in hotel management.

24

Information technology

| From: Larry Smith |
| To: Alvin Green |
| Subject: Visit and hotel |

Hi Alvin!

Thanks for your last email and the **attachment** with the slides for your talk. I think it's best if you bring your own laptop for the presentation, and also a **cable** in case you need to **charge** it. Remember that you'll need a different kind of **plug** over here in the UK.

I know you'll want to be able to access the online **database** while you're over here. That shouldn't be a problem, as your hotel has **broadband**. They will give you a code that allows you to **log in**.

Looking forward to seeing you next week!

Larry

I don't know how I managed before we had computers! I use mine every day. I spend hours just **browsing**, though I also have all my favourite sites saved as **bookmarks**.

I love playing **virtual reality** games. I also use my laptop for watching TV, and I enjoy using the **interactive** features. I have all my photos **stored** on my computer too. I've just got a new **application** that helps me edit them.

Last year I had a disaster when my computer **crashed**, and I didn't have my files **backed up**. I've learned my lesson now, and as well as making backups, I **run** anti-virus software regularly.

Word Finder

application	NOUN	In computing, an **application** is a piece of software designed to carry out a particular task.
attachment	NOUN	In computing, an **attachment** is a file that is attached separately to a message that you send to someone.
back up	PHRASAL VERB	If you **back up** your work on a computer, you make an electronic copy of it.
bookmark	NOUN	In computing, a **bookmark** is the address of an Internet site that you put into a list on your computer so that you can return to it easily.
broadband	NOUN	**Broadband** is a method of sending many electronic messages at the same time, using a wide range of frequencies.

browse	VERB	If you **browse** on a computer, you search for information in computer files or on the Internet, especially on the World Wide Web.
burn	VERB	To **burn** a CD-ROM means to write or copy data onto it.
cable	NOUN	A **cable** is a thick wire, or a group of wires inside a rubber or plastic covering, which is used to carry electricity or electronic signals.
charge	VERB	If you **charge** a piece of equipment, you put electricity into it.
crash	VERB	If a computer or a computer program **crashes**, it fails suddenly.
database	NOUN	A **database** is a collection of data that is stored in a computer and that can easily be used and added to.
experiment	NOUN	An **experiment** is a scientific test which is done in order to discover what happens to something in particular conditions.
interactive	ADJECTIVE	An **interactive** computer program or television system is one that allows direct communication between the user and the machine.
log in	PHRASAL VERB	When someone **logs in**, they start using a computer system, usually by typing their name and password.
log off / out	PHRASAL VERB	When someone **logs off** or **logs out**, they stop using a computer system by typing a particular command.
plug	NOUN	A **plug** on a piece of electrical equipment is a small plastic object with two or three metal pins that fit into the holes of an electric socket and connects the equipment to the electricity supply.
run	VERB	If you **run** a computer program or other process, you start it and let it continue.
signal	NOUN	A **signal** is a series of radio waves, light waves, or changes in electrical current which may carry information.
store	VERB	When you **store** information, you keep it in your memory, in a file, or in a computer.
virtual reality	NOUN	**Virtual reality** is an environment that is produced by a computer and seems very like reality to the person experiencing it.
wire	NOUN	A **wire** is a cable that carries power or signals from one place to another.

Exercise 1

Complete the sentences by writing one word or phrase in each gap.

| virtual reality | database | broadband | attachment | bookmarks | application |

1 The information is all stored in a _____.
2 I found a great free photo-editing _____.
3 Could you send me that document as an _____?
4 You can just transfer your _____ if you change computers.
5 You really need high-speed _____ to play these games.
6 _____ is an artificial environment created with software which the user experiences as a real environment.

UNIT 24 Information technology

Exercise 2
Rearrange the letters to find words. Use the definitions to help you.
1 cabk pu _____ (to make a copy of a computer file which you can use if the original file is damaged or lost)
2 serowb _____ (to look at websites on the Internet)
3 racheg _____ (to put electricity into the battery of a piece of electrical equipment, such as a mobile phone)
4 srachse _____ (if a computer or a computer program does this, it fails suddenly)
5 gol ni _____ (to type in your unique details, usually a username and password, to start using a computer or website)
6 resot _____ (to keep information on a computer)
7 unr _____ (to start a computer program)
8 rubn _____ (to copy data onto a CD-ROM or DVD-ROM)

Exercise 3
Match the two parts together.
1 You need to back up
2 I'll burn
3 I wanted to call you but I couldn't get a signal
4 I need to charge
5 My computer's crashed again.
6 If you're not logged in,

a my phone. It's nearly out of battery.
b I can't get it to do anything.
c on my mobile phone.
d your files regularly.
e these photos onto a disk for you if you like.
f you can't see the photos.

Exercise 4
Put each sentence into the correct order.
1 She / experiment to / prove / performed an / her theory /.
_____
2 An interactive / you the / tutorial teaches / the software / basics of /.
_____
3 on the / Double-click / run / it / program icon to / .
_____
4 a special / I need / connect my / phone to / cable to / my computer /.
_____
5 that there / loose / Check / wires / are no /.
_____
6 where I / can plug / Is there / this in / a socket / ?
_____

25

Services

Treetops HOTEL

For a great break, and the ultimate in **hospitality**, come to the *Treetops Hotel!*

Treat yourself to a few days of luxury at the *Treetops Hotel!* We are here to look after you, and our **customer service** is second to none. All the food in our restaurants is prepared by top chefs, and **room service** is available any time of the day or night. Make sure you **take advantage** of all the hotel's **facilities**, such as our beautiful swimming pool and spa.

Should you wish to go sightseeing, we can arrange guides to take you off the usual **tourist trail** and show you the hidden treasures of the area. **Standards** of spoken English are high, and for your **convenience**, meals are provided as part of the tours.

My mum has been having trouble with her heart. She went to her **GP surgery** several times, but the doctor said there was nothing wrong. Then one day, she collapsed and we had to call an ambulance. The **paramedics** were great, and dealt with her calmly and efficiently.

At hospital, the **consultant** did some tests and said that she needed to have an operation. Luckily, she had **private health care** so she was able to stay on a **private ward**, which was almost like a hotel. She's made a good recovery, but still has to go back once a month as an **outpatient** to get checked over.

Word Finder

bank account	NOUN A **bank account** is an arrangement with a bank that allows you to keep your money in the bank and to take some out when you need it.
compulsory education	NOUN **Compulsory education** is the period of education when young people have to be at school by law.
consultant	1 NOUN A **consultant** is a person who gives expert advice to a person or organization on a particular subject. 2 NOUN A **consultant** is an experienced doctor with a high position, who specializes in one area of medicine.
convenience	NOUN **Convenience** is the quality of being easy or useful for a particular purpose.
customer service	NOUN **Customer service** refers to the way that companies behave towards their customers, for example how well they treat them.

UNIT 25 Services

Word Finder

deposit	NOUN A **deposit** is a sum of money that is part of the full price of something, and which you pay when you agree to buy it.
facilities	NOUN **Facilities** are buildings, pieces of equipment, or services that are provided for a particular purpose.
food outlet	NOUN A **food outlet** is a place where prepared food is sold.
GP surgery	NOUN A **GP surgery** is a place where doctors who treat all types of illness work.
hospitality	NOUN **Hospitality** is friendly, welcoming behaviour towards guests or people you have just met.
natural history museum	NOUN A **natural history museum** is a museum that displays items to do with animals, plants and the natural world.
outpatient	NOUN An **outpatient** is someone who receives treatment at a hospital but does not spend the night there.
paramedic	NOUN A **paramedic** is a person whose training is similar to that of a nurse and who helps to do medical work.
private health care	NOUN **Private health care** is medical treatment that you have to pay for.
private ward	NOUN A **private ward** in a hospital is a room where patients who are paying for their treatment stay.
room service	NOUN **Room service** is a service in a hotel where guests can order food and drinks to have in their rooms.
safe	NOUN A **safe** is a strong metal cupboard with special locks, in which you keep money, jewellery, or other valuable things.
standard	NOUN A **standard** is a level of quality or achievement, especially a level that is thought to be acceptable.
take advantage of	PHRASE If someone **takes advantage of** you, they treat you unfairly for their own benefit.
tourist trail	NOUN The **tourist trail** is the places that visitors to a place usually go to.

Exercise 1

For each question, tick the correct answer.

1 Which of these do you find in a hospital?
   - ❏ GP surgery
   - ❏ private healthcare
   - ❏ private ward

2 Which of these people drives an ambulance?
   - ❏ a consultant
   - ❏ a paramedic
   - ❏ an outpatient

3 Guests often comment on their hosts'
   - ❏ hospitality.
   - ❏ convenience.
   - ❏ facilities.

4 Where do you leave valuables in a hotel?
   - ❏ a safe
   - ❏ a deposit
   - ❏ a bank account

5 How can you get something to eat in a hotel?
   - ❏ food outlet
   - ❏ room service
   - ❏ customer service

95

Exercise 2

Choose the correct word or phrase.

1 A **private ward / GP surgery** is where you go to see a doctor.
2 All children in the UK stay in **compulsory education / hospitality** until the age of 16.
3 A **consultant / paramedic** is someone who gives expert advice.
4 Here's a map of the **tourist trail / facilities**. Enjoy your sightseeing!
5 Dinosaur bones are often on display at a **private ward / natural history museum**.
6 High **standards / facilities** of cleanliness are required in hospitals.

Exercise 3

Put the correct word or phrase in each gap.

| consultant | private ward | GP surgery | outpatients |
| hospitality | facilities | paramedic | private healthcare |

I wanted to be a ¹_____ when I was younger, but now I think I'd like to be a doctor instead. I'd probably start off at a ²_____ getting some general experience, but later I'd like to be a ³_____, specializing in bones. I'd prefer to work in ⁴_____, but I'm not bothered as long as I get a job. I wouldn't mind working at my local hospital. The ⁵_____ are great for patients and ⁶_____.

Exercise 4

Rearrange the letters to find words. Use the definitions to help you.

1 smercuto vcersie _____ (when someone helps you, for example in a shop or hotel)
2 dofo letout _____ (a kind of shop where you can buy food)
3 posdeit _____ (a payment you make when you want to buy something – you might get it back later)
4 ecnoveeinnc _____ (something that makes life easier)
5 siiltiface _____ (buildings, equipment and services for a particular purpose)
6 opniettatu _____ (a patient who gets treatment in hospital, but doesn't need to stay overnight)

Exercise 5

Which sentences are correct?

1 No one likes to be taken advantage of. ☐
2 Standard of private healthcare have risen recently. ☐
3 I left my passport in the hotel safe, but it's been stolen! ☐
4 I saw a beautiful painting in the natural history museum. I love art exhibitions. ☐
5 You need to open a bank account before you can deposit money. ☐
6 I ordered a delicious meal from customer service. ☐

26

People

> **Adventurous** woman, 23, seeks **enthusiastic** companion for travel. Must be **bright** and **ambitious**, as well as **appreciating** the finer things in life!

> **Well-built** man, 31, seeks kind and **responsible** woman to love and **admire**. I am a **cautious** person, but the right woman will find me **generous** and **caring**.

My best friend is the well-known guitarist, Dan Karlsson. Dan is tall, with **wavy** black hair and a huge grin. His health is not very good, and he often looks **pale**, but he is **amused** by the fact that his thin **features** are seen as attractive by many women. He once told me he had been **astonished** to receive a love letter from a very famous actress, but that he was too much of a **coward** to call her!

addicted	ADJECTIVE	Someone who is **addicted** to a harmful drug cannot stop taking it.
admire	VERB	If you **admire** someone or something, you like and respect them very much.
adventurous	ADJECTIVE	Someone who is **adventurous** is willing to take risks and to try new methods.
aggressive	ADJECTIVE	An **aggressive** person has a quality of anger and determination that makes them ready to attack other people.
ambitious	ADJECTIVE	Someone who is **ambitious** has a strong desire to be successful, rich, or powerful.
amused	ADJECTIVE	If you are **amused** by something, it makes you want to laugh or smile.
appreciate	VERB	If you **appreciate** something that someone has done for you or is going to do for you, you are grateful for it.
astonished	ADJECTIVE	If you are **astonished** by something, you are very surprised by it.
bright	ADJECTIVE	If you describe someone as **bright**, you mean that they are quick at learning new things.
caring	ADJECTIVE	If someone is **caring**, they are affectionate, helpful, and sympathetic.

cautious	ADJECTIVE	Someone who is **cautious** acts very carefully in order to avoid possible danger.
coward	NOUN	If you call someone a **coward**, you disapprove of them because they are easily frightened and avoid dangerous or difficult situations.
enthusiastic	ADJECTIVE	If you are **enthusiastic** about something, you show how much you like or enjoy it by the way that you behave and talk.
feature	NOUN	Your **features** are your eyes, nose, mouth, and other parts of your face.
generous	ADJECTIVE	A **generous** person gives more of something, especially money, than is usual or expected.
pale	ADJECTIVE	If something is **pale**, it is very light in colour or almost white.
plump	ADJECTIVE	You can describe someone or something as **plump** to indicate that they are rather fat or rounded.
responsible	ADJECTIVE	If you are **responsible** for something, it is your job or duty to deal with it and make decisions relating to it.
wavy	ADJECTIVE	**Wavy** hair is not straight or curly, but curves slightly.
well-built	ADJECTIVE	A **well-built** person, especially a man, has quite a big body and quite large muscles.

Exercise 1
Choose the correct word.

My friend Anne

As a young woman, my friend Anne was very ¹**amused / pale / adventurous** and she travelled all over the world. She met a woman who was planning to set up a school in a rural African village. Anne was very ²**enthusiastic / aggressive / generous** about the idea, and agreed to go and help her.

At the school, Anne was ³**caring / responsible / addicted** for teaching English. I think the children must have been ⁴**aggressive / cautious / astonished** to meet this tiny woman with red hair and very ⁵**bright / pale / plump** skin!

Anne worked at the school for four years, and I really ⁶**admire / appreciate / care** her for that.

Exercise 2
Rearrange the letters to find words. Use the definitions to help you.

1 usbmiotai _____ (having a strong wish to be successful)
2 souaticu _____ (very careful to avoid risks)
3 masude _____ (finding something funny)
4 renseguo _____ (happy to give people money, time or things)
5 lwel-tlbiu _____ (having a large, muscular body)
6 muppl _____ (a little overweight)

Work on your Vocabulary Upper Intermediate (B2)

UNIT 26 People

Exercise 3

Match the sentence halves.

1 He was a tall man
2 Like many aggressive people,
3 She was adopted by
4 He was addicted to junk food and
5 My ideas make her nervous because she
6 He has dark, wavy hair

a a very caring family.
b is rather cautious by nature.
c had become rather plump.
d with thin, sharp features.
e and a pale complexion.
f he is really a coward.

Exercise 4

Decide if the pairs of sentences have similar meanings.

1 **A** Jake's quick temper and thoughtlessness make him ready to attack other people.
  B Jake is aggressive.
2 **A** Jake needs extra help at school if he is to do well.
  B Jake is quite bright and is likely to do well at school.
3 **A** Jake has a responsible attitude towards his pet dog.
  B Jake looks after his pet dog well.
4 **A** Jake is very keen on sport, and plays football as often as he gets the chance.
  B Jake plays football as often as he can because he's enthusiastic about sport.
5 **A** Jake doesn't always appreciate the problems he causes for his parents.
  B Jake doesn't like causing problems for his parents.

Exercise 5

Complete the sentences by writing one word in each gap.

| generous | astonished | bright | amused | wavy | plump |

1 She has _____, shoulder-length hair.
2 She kissed the baby's _____ cheeks.
3 Thank you for your extremely _____ gift.
4 Paul was laughing, but his mother didn't look _____.
5 I was absolutely _____ when I heard that I had won the competition.
6 Of course your hand is burned after you picked up the hot baking tray without an oven glove – now that wasn't very _____, was it?

Exercise 6

Choose the correct word to fill each gap.

1 Our most **addicted / astonished / ambitious** students often take extra classes.
2 He is far too **cautious / ambitious / adventurous** to be really successful in business.
3 I have always **wanted / admired / looked forward to** Gemma's determination to succeed.
4 Jon has always been very **responsible / enthusiastic / generous** towards his friends.
5 Going to work in a safari park was a very **aggressive / adventurous / astonished** thing to do.
6 Peter was very **adventurous / enthusiastic / ambitious** about the idea of setting up our own business.

99

27

Seeing, hearing, touching, smelling and tasting

Jamie I'm looking for another job. I hate working in the soup factory. It **stinks**, and the noise of the machines is **deafening**.

Alex Your work sounds really **monotonous** too. It must drive you crazy!

Jamie It does, and not just me. One of the guys started **yelling** at the manager the other day, and **grabbed** him by his shirt collar.

Alex And what happened?

Jamie Well everyone was **staring** at them, thinking there was going to be a huge fight, but then they calmed down. The boss took it really seriously, though, asking for **witnesses** to come forward to tell him what had happened.

We had a great meal at Luciano's last night. First we had some cocktails. I tried to **sip** mine slowly, because it was quite strong! It had limes in it, which gave it a lovely **sour** taste. We both had steak for our main course. It had a really good **flavour**.

At one point, Dominic **whispered** to me to look who had just come in. I **glanced** towards the door just in time to **catch a glimpse** of Holly Bright, the politician, before she was taken off to a private room. I **overheard** one of the waiters saying that she was a very demanding customer!

Word Finder

catch a glimpse	PHRASE	If you **catch a glimpse** of someone or something, you see them briefly and not very well.
deafening	ADJECTIVE	A **deafening** noise is a very loud noise.
flavour	NOUN	The **flavour** of a food or drink is its taste.
flavourful	ADJECTIVE	Food or drink that is **flavourful** has a strong, good taste.
flavourless	ADJECTIVE	Food or drink that is **flavourless** is not good because it does not have enough taste.
fluffy	ADJECTIVE	If you describe something such as a towel or a toy animal as **fluffy**, you mean that it is very soft.
glance	VERB	If you **glance** at something or someone, you look at them very quickly and then look away again immediately.
grab	VERB	If you **grab** something, you take it or pick it up suddenly and roughly.
monotonous	ADJECTIVE	Something that is **monotonous** is very boring because it has a regular, repeated pattern that never changes.
overhear	VERB	If you **overhear** someone, you hear what they are saying when they are not talking to you and they do not know that you are listening.

Work on your Vocabulary Upper Intermediate (B2)

UNIT 27 Seeing, hearing, touching, smelling and tasting

rotten	ADJECTIVE If food, wood, or another substance is **rotten**, it has decayed and can no longer be used.
scan	VERB When you **scan** something, you look over it quickly.
scented	ADJECTIVE **Scented** things have a pleasant smell, either naturally or because perfume has been added to them.
sharp	ADJECTIVE A **sharp** point or edge is very thin and can cut through things very easily. A sharp knife, tool, or other object has a point or edge of this kind.
sip	VERB If you **sip** a drink, you drink by taking just a small amount at a time.
sour	ADJECTIVE Something that is **sour** has a sharp taste, like the taste of a lemon or lime.
spectator	NOUN A **spectator** is someone who watches something, especially a sporting event.
stare	VERB If you **stare** at someone or something, you look at them for a long time.
stink	VERB To **stink** means to smell extremely unpleasant.
whisper	VERB When you **whisper**, you say something very quietly, using your breath rather than your throat, so that only people very close to you can hear you.
witness	NOUN A **witness** to an event such as an accident or crime is a person who saw it.
yell	VERB If you **yell**, you shout loudly, usually because you are excited, angry, or in pain.

Exercise 1

Are the highlighted words correct or incorrect in the sentences?

1 Was that Mary just going through the door? I only caught a **stare** ❑ of her and am not sure.
2 Please turn that music down! The sound is **deafening** ❑.
3 This food is completely **flavourful** ❑. It needs some salt and pepper.
4 This cuddly toy is so soft and **fluffy** ❑ to the touch. We must buy it for the baby.
5 The apples you bought are **rotten** ❑ and you should throw them away.
6 Have you seen these **stinking** ❑ soaps? They smell heavenly.

Exercise 2

Write the missing words in sentence B so that it means the same as sentence A.

1 **A** If you don't want anybody to know what you're going to say, why don't you say it quietly in my ear?
   B If you don't want anybody to know what you're going to say, why don't you _____ it in my ear?

2 **A** Don't shout so loudly across the street, Philip. It's not good manners.
   B Don't _____ across the street, Philip. It's bad manners.

3 **A** This milk smells very bad. It has gone sour.
   B This milk _____. It has gone sour.

4 **A** All the people watching the match shouted together when Freddy scored the goal.
   B All the _____ shouted together when Freddy scored the goal.

101

Exercise 3
Complete the sentences by writing one word in each gap.
1 Jenny was a _____ to a car accident that happened outside her flat. She has been asked to go to the police station and tell them what she saw.
2 Don't _____ at people like that, Johnny. It's impolite.
3 Phil's voice always makes me want to fall sleep. It is so _____.
4 The coffee is very hot, I'm afraid. You will have to _____ it slowly till it cools down.
5 Irene _____ the page quickly but couldn't see the contact details for the opticians in town.
6 I love to light _____ candles in the house after I've been cooking. They remove cooking odours really quickly.

Exercise 4
Find the words or phrases that do not belong, as shown.
1 Words to do with looking
   scan   glance   stare   catch a glimpse   witness   (sharp)   spectator
2 Words to do with smells
   fluffy   stink   sour   scented   rotten
3 Words to do with speech
   deafening   monotonous   sip   whisper   yell

Exercise 5
Choose the correct word.
1 I **listened / overheard / spoke** two people on the bus talking about a concert in the neighbourhood. I wonder where it could be.
2 Officer! That man just **grabbed / removed / captured** my handbag!
3 These kitchen knives are so **soft / strong / sharp**, I'm afraid to use them.
4 I know we said we would go to the cinema, but I **glimpsed / stared / scanned** the film pages in the newspaper and there is nothing on.
5 This chicken has a lovely **scent / flavour / stink**. What spices have you used?

28 Movement and speed

Peter I wonder why Greg was **in a hurry** this morning? He came **flying** into the kitchen as though someone was chasing him!

Suzi He's been told that he'll be fired if he's late for work any more. He used to get a lift to work with Andy, but since Andy **moved away**, he's had to walk, and he keeps being late.

Peter Poor Greg! I completely understand – I find it very difficult to **get moving** in the morning, but I hate having to **rush** my breakfast.

Suzi Me too! A relaxed cup of coffee and a croissant, then a gentle **stroll** to the bus stop – that's how I like to start my day.

I've always loved physical activity. When I was young, I used to belong to the army cadets, and I really enjoyed **marching**. Nowadays, I run for an athletics club.

We had a big competition last week. I've had some injuries, so I always make sure I **stretch** a lot before **racing**. I wasn't expecting to win, but in the last lap I suddenly realized it was possible, and I had just enough energy to lengthen my **stride** and **speed up**, just as the others were getting tired. Winning that race was just fantastic!

My girlfriend complains that I never sit still. Even when I'm not running, I love **hiking** in the mountains, and in the summer we went **trekking** in Nepal.

Word Finder

dash	1 VERB If you **dash** somewhere, you run or go there quickly and suddenly. 2 NOUN A **dash** is a quick run somewhere.
come / go flying	VERB If you say that someone **comes** or **goes flying** somewhere, you mean that they move somewhere extremely quickly.
get moving	PHRASE If you need to **get moving**, you need to hurry.
hike	NOUN A **hike** is a long walk in the country, especially one that you go on for pleasure.
hurry	VERB If you **hurry** somewhere, you go there as quickly as you can.
in a hurry	PHRASE If someone is **in a hurry**, they are trying to do something or get somewhere as fast as possible.
keep your speed up	PHRASE If you **keep your speed up**, you keep going at the same, fast rate.
march	VERB When soldiers **march** somewhere, they walk there with regular steps.
movable	ADJECTIVE Something that is **movable** can be moved from one place or position to another.
move away	PHRASAL VERB If someone **moves away**, they go to live in a different place.
move into	PHRASAL VERB If someone **moves into** a home or an area, they go to live there.

Word Finder

move out of	PHRASAL VERB	If someone **moves out of** a home or an area, they stop living there and go to live somewhere else.
movement	NOUN	**Movement** involves changing position or going from one place to another.
race	VERB	If you **race** somewhere, you go there as quickly as possible.
rush	VERB	If you **rush** something, you do it in a hurry, often too quickly and without much care.
speed of sound	NOUN	The **speed of sound** is the speed at which sound travels.
speed up	PHRASAL VERB	If someone or something **speeds up**, they get faster.
stretch	VERB	When you **stretch**, you put your arms or legs out straight and tighten your muscles.
stride	NOUN	A **stride** is a long step which you take when you are walking or running.
stroll	NOUN	A **stroll** is a slow, relaxed walk.
trek	VERB	If you **trek** somewhere, you go on a journey across difficult country, usually on foot.

Exercise 1

Match the sentence halves.

1 When the fire alarm sounded
2 Sorry, I can't stop and chat,
3 After I had been sitting studying all day,
4 There's a movable screen here
5 We started out at dawn on our trek
6 The car seemed to speed up

a that divides up the office space.
b through the mountains.
c I'm in a hurry.
d there was a mad dash for the exit.
e after it went round the corner.
f I needed to stretch my legs.

Exercise 2

Which sentences are correct?

1 The French cyclist seemed to speed up at the end of the race and that's why he won. ❑
2 I was at such a hurry to catch the bus that I forgot to lock the door. ❑
3 Fast runners usually have a long stride. ❑
4 The journey took ages because once we left the motorway it was impossible to set our speed up. ❑
5 After running a marathon, it's important to strain your leg muscles. ❑
6 The soldiers marched through the town as part of the ceremony. ❑

UNIT 28 Movement and speed

Exercise 3

Put the correct word in each gap.

| sound | hurry | dash | stroll | hike | race |

Hi Jim

I've just spent a weekend at a special football training camp. It was a nightmare. First of all, I got up late and had to ¹_____ to the station to get the 7.30 train. The guy doing the training was really tough. The first thing we had to do was ²_____ each other and he joined in too – and I can tell you he could run at the speed of ³_____! Even when he was just speaking he seemed to be in a ⁴_____. On Sunday we went on a long ⁵_____ in the mountains. The trainer was good, though, because he made us all do some stretching exercises at the end of the day so that we won't be so stiff tomorrow. I don't think I'll do anything tomorrow – not even go for a ⁶_____ in the park.

See you

George

Exercise 4

Choose the correct word or phrase.
1 If you don't **get / become / act** moving, we'll miss the bus.
2 Sorry, I must **jump / fly / hike**, my train leaves in five minutes.
3 On Sunday afternoon, we had a leisurely **stroll / journey / voyage** in the park.
4 This plane can travel at twice the speed of **noise / loudness / sound**.
5 Don't **skip / rush / push** your homework, you'll only make mistakes.
6 A new family have **moved away / moved into / moved back** our block of flats.

Exercise 5

Are the highlighted words correct or incorrect in the sentences?
1 This plane can travel faster than the speed of **noise** ❏.
2 He told me to hurry **out** ❏ and that I always did everything too slowly.
3 We're going to move **away** ❏ from the city and go and live in the countryside.
4 The couple enjoyed a romantic **stroll** ❏ on the beach at sunset.
5 Can't we go to our local restaurant? It's such a **trek** ❏ to go to the city centre.
6 I knew I was going to be sick so I **marched** ❏ to the toilets.

105

29 Phrases with *be*, *do*, *get*, *have* and *make*

When we were younger, we used to **make fun of** a girl in our class called Wendi. I think it was something **to do with** the fact that her parents were doctors, and she had a really upper-class accent compared to us. **To make matters worse**, she was extremely clever, and the teachers all loved her.

I've often thought about that girl and wondered what happened to her. That sort of teasing can really **do damage**, and I **do** think the school should have done more to protect her. I feel so guilty about it, but I don't suppose there's anything I can do to **make up for** my behaviour now.

Evie Why don't you come to the gym with me, Lara? It would **do you good**.

Lara I know, but I'm hopeless at that sort of thing. I'm scared I'd **make a fool of** myself.

Evie I'm sure you wouldn't. The equipment's so easy to use, you'd soon **get used to** using it. And we're lucky to have a free gym while we're students. We should really **make the most of** it!

Lara Yes, that **makes sense**. I'll think about it.

Good to know!

Many verbs, such as be, do, get, have and make have lots of different meanings. Often they are used in phrases. In these cases, it is best to learn the whole phrase. Common verbs like make and do often have many associated phrasal verbs, which you need to learn as separate items.

be / have to do with something	PHRASE If one thing **has** or **is** something **to do with** another, the two things are connected.
do	VERB **Do** is used before another verb to add emphasis in a sentence.
do damage / harm	PHRASE If something **does damage** or **does harm** to something, it damages or harms it.
do someone good	PHRASE If something **does** you **good**, it benefits you or makes you feel better.

Work on your Vocabulary Upper Intermediate (B2)

UNIT 29 Phrases with *be, do, get, have* and *make*

do up	PHRASAL VERB If you **do up** an old building, you decorate it and repair it.
be / have to do with something	PHRASE If one thing **has** or **is something to do with** another, the two things are connected.
do without	PHRASAL VERB If you **do without** something, you are able to manage without having it.
get used to	PHRASE If you **get used to** something, you become familiar with it so that it does not seem difficult or surprising.
make	VERB If you **make** money, you get it by working for it, by selling something, or by winning it.
make a fool (out) of yourself	PHRASE If you **make a fool of yourself**, you do something that makes other people think you are foolish.
make a loss	PHRASE If someone **makes a loss**, they end up with less money than they started with.
make a profit	PHRASE If someone **makes a profit**, they end up with more money than they started with.
make for	PHRASAL VERB If you **make for** a particular place, you start going towards it.
make fun of	PHRASE If you **make fun of** someone or something, you laugh at them, tease them, or make jokes about them.
to make matters worse	PHRASE You say **to make matters worse** when you are going to talk about something that happened that made a bad situation even worse.
make out	PHRASAL VERB If you **make out** that something is true, you try to make people believe that it is true.
make sense	1 PHRASE If something **makes sense**, it is sensible or it is the right thing to do. 2 PHRASE If something such as a piece of writing or speech **makes sense**, it means something.
make into	PHRASAL VERB If you **make** one thing **into** another, you change it so that it becomes the second thing.
make the most / best of	PHRASE If you **make the most of** something or **make the best of** something, you enjoy it as much as you can.
make up	PHRASAL VERB If you **make** something **up**, you invent it.
make up for	PHRASAL VERB To **make up for** a bad experience or the loss of something means to make the situation better or make the person involved happier.

Word Finder

Exercise 1
Complete the sentences by writing one phrase in each gap.

| make sense | make matters worse | make a loss | make up for |
| make fun of | make up | make a profit |

1 I'd left my train ticket at home and to _____, I didn't have enough money on me to buy another ticket.
2 This machine looks so complicated, it would _____ to study the instruction manual before doing anything else.
3 Despite selling lots of tickets to the concert, the organizers didn't _____ because the expenses were so high.
4 It isn't a great job, but the short hours and good salary will _____ that.
5 It isn't fair to _____ somebody because they don't dress in the latest fashion.
6 If they can't admit the real reason why they're late, they'll have to _____ an excuse.

Exercise 2
Decide if the pairs of sentences have the same meaning.

1 A You'd benefit from spending a few days relaxing at the seaside.
  B It'd do you good to spend a few days relaxing at the seaside. ❏
2 A Jill has got used to taking her dog for a walk before she goes to work.
  B Jill has stopped taking her dog for a walk before she goes to work. ❏
3 A Tony made a fortune from designing software.
  B The software that Tony designed earned him a lot of money. ❏
4 A My company buys houses and does them up before selling them.
  B My company builds new houses then sells them. ❏
5 A If I'm going out for lunch, I usually do without breakfast.
  B I don't usually eat breakfast if I'm going out for lunch. ❏

Exercise 3
Write the missing phrases in sentence B so that it means the same as sentence A.

1 A Nigel bought an old farmhouse and spent months repairing and decorating it.
  B Nigel bought an old farmhouse and spent months _____.
2 A I don't understand why there are no clues as to how the necklace was stolen.
  B It _____ that there are no clues as to how the necklace was stolen.
3 A A lot of former factories have been converted into flats in the last few years.
  B A lot of former factories have been _____ flats in the last few years.
4 A Manufacturing creates jobs, but is bad for the environment.
  B Manufacturing creates jobs, but it _____ to the environment.

Exercise 4
Match the two parts.
1. gain money
2. go in the direction of
3. make jokes about
4. state something that isn't true
5. compensate for

a. make out
b. make for
c. make
d. make fun of
e. make up for

Exercise 5
Which sentences are correct?
1. Deal with it yourself. It's got nothing to do with me. ☐
2. I see what you mean, but I do think you're jumping to conclusions. ☐
3. I know it's a shock at first, but you'll soon get used to be famous. ☐
4. I stood up and made for the door, but Rick reached it first. ☐
5. The writing's so faint, I can hardly make up what it says. ☐
6. I can't do without a bit of time to myself every day. ☐

Exercise 6
Are the highlighted words correct or incorrect in the sentences?
1. Suri **made a fool of herself** ☐ by refusing to join the team.
2. It **makes matters bad** ☐ that you won't even apologize.
3. It **makes sense** ☐ to check there are rooms available at the hotel before we book tickets for the opera.
4. This is your only chance to go to the seaside, so **make the most of it** ☐.
5. They had an argument but they **made it out** ☐ very soon.
6. In her new job, she **makes up** ☐ far more than she used to earn.

30

Metaphorical language

A metaphor is an imaginative way of describing something by referring to something else that is the same in a particular way. For example, if you want to say that someone is very shy and frightened of things, you might say that they are a mouse. In this unit, you learn other words that are often used with a metaphorical meaning.

> I had been having a lot of problems at work. My boss had a really **fiery** temper, and was very difficult to work for. The company began doing worse and worse and life became very stressful indeed. I had lots of ideas, but my boss just **shot** them **down** immediately. To make things worse, the area I worked in was a legal **minefield**, and I was constantly worried about breaking the law.
>
> It was during this time that my friend suggested I take up yoga in order to relax. I found that it really **lifted** my spirits. When the company eventually **collapsed**, I decided to retrain as a yoga teacher. I had never imagined my **career path** going in this direction, but life sometimes **takes an unexpected turn**, doesn't it?

> I decided to write this book because I wanted to tell my father's story to the world. He had never spoken about his experiences in the war, often **burying** his memories of it, but I had a **gut feeling** that he had been involved in something exceptional.
>
> After his death, I managed to **dig up** lots of information from newspapers, libraries and family letters. Then, quite unexpectedly, my uncle gave me a diary that my father had written.
>
> My father rarely spoke about his experiences in the war, but I always knew they were a great **burden** to him. He did his best to **mask** his feelings of despair afterwards, but he had a lot of problems and found it hard to hold down a job. My mother had to do everything, and at times it was difficult for us as a family to **keep our heads above water**.

Word Finder

blackout	NOUN If a **blackout** is imposed on a particular piece of news, journalists are prevented from broadcasting or publishing it.
burden	NOUN If you describe a problem or a responsibility as a **burden**, you mean that it causes someone a lot of difficulty, worry, or hard work.
bury	VERB If you **bury** a feeling, you try not to show it.
by ear	PHRASE If you play music **by ear**, you do not read music as you play.
by heart	PHRASE If you learn something **by heart**, you learn it so that you can remember it without reading it.

UNIT 30 Metaphorical language

Word Finder

career path	NOUN Someone's **career path** is the way that their jobs change and develop.
collapse	VERB If something **collapses**, it fails or comes to an end completely and suddenly.
cross your mind	PHRASE If a thought **crosses your mind**, you think of it.
dig up	PHRASAL VERB If you **dig up** information or facts, you discover something that has not previously been widely known.
drag	VERB If a period of time or an event **drags**, it is very boring and seems to last a long time.
fiery	ADJECTIVE If you describe someone as **fiery**, you mean that they show very strong emotions, especially anger.
gut feeling	NOUN A **gut feeling** is based on instinct or emotion rather than on reason.
keep your head above water	PHRASE If you **keep your head above water**, you just manage to avoid difficulties, especially financial difficulties.
leak	VERB If a secret document or piece of information is **leaked**, someone lets the public know about it.
lift your spirits	PHRASE If something **lifts your spirits**, it makes you feel happier.
mask	VERB If you **mask** your feelings, you deliberately do not show them in your behaviour, so that people cannot know what you really feel.
minefield	NOUN If you describe a situation as a **minefield**, you are emphasizing that there are a lot of hidden dangers or problems.
plant	VERB If you **plant** an idea in someone's mind, they begin to accept the idea without realizing that it has originally come from you and not from them.
shoot down	PHRASAL VERB If you **shoot down** someone's ideas, you say or show them that they are completely wrong.
take an unexpected turn	PHRASE If your life **takes an unexpected turn**, something happens that you did not expect.

Exercise 1

Match the sentence halves.

1 I didn't expect her to shoot down
2 There's a total news blackout
3 Did your lawyers do a good job of negotiating
4 Do you think you could dig up
5 The grandmother has the full
6 When I got an A grade in my exam,

a my idea like that without any discussion.
b it really lifted my spirits.
c the minefield of clauses in the contract?
d from the region.
e some background facts about this company?
f burden of looking after the children.

Exercise 2

Choose the correct word.

1 My career took an unexpected **way / turn / route** when I moved to Europe.
2 The information about the royal family was **uncovered / dripped / leaked** to the press by one of their drivers.
3 Once she'd **planted / rooted / stemmed** the idea of changing career in my mind, I couldn't think of anything else.
4 I'm so busy revising for my exam and doing a part-time job, it's hard to keep my head above **chin / level / water**.
5 Time really **drags / passes / lengthens** when you've got nothing to do.
6 What's your **heart / head / gut** feeling about Conrad? Do you trust him?

Exercise 3

Find the words or phrases that do not belong, as shown.

1 Bury	feelings	treasure	~~rules~~
2 Learn	by heart	by hand	by yourself
3 Plant	a wish	an idea	a shrub
4 Leak	oil	anger	information
5 Lift	spirits	weights	savings
6 Mask	a comparison	the truth	feelings

Exercise 4

Which sentences are correct?

1 Peace talks have collapsed and the government representatives have returned home. ❏
2 He doesn't need sheet music; he can play by hand. ❏
3 I haven't really decided on a career path yet. ❏
4 The information about the singer's whereabouts was drained to the press by a so-called friend. ❏
5 It never made up my mind that you might want to come too. Sorry! ❏
6 There's no need to shoot down the idea straight away. Think about it for a moment. ❏

UNIT 30 Metaphorical language

Exercise 5

Put the correct word in each gap.

| gut | burden | minefield | fiery | crossed | plant | bury | heated |

Hi Jennie

I hate to ¹_____ you with my worries, but I'm a bit concerned about my son. He's 15 now and has started to ²_____ his feelings. He never tells me anything anymore and I've got a ³_____ feeling that he's not as happy as he used to be. It's ⁴_____ my mind that he might be worried about his exams, or perhaps he's got a girlfriend. What do you think? Trying to talk to him is like walking through a ⁵_____. First he says nothing, then he suddenly gets angry, but he never used to have a ⁶_____ temper. Do you think this is just typical teenage behaviour?

Love

Suzi

Exercise 6

Decide if the pairs of sentences have the same meaning.

1. **A** Getting the news really lifted my spirits. ☐
   B Getting the news really dampened my spirits.
2. **A** You shouldn't try to mask your feelings like that. ☐
   B You shouldn't try to hide your feelings like that.
3. **A** Time really dragged on that ten-hour flight. ☐
   B Time passed quickly on that ten-hour flight.
4. **A** Did Marie always have such a fiery temper? ☐
   B Has Marie always had such a short temper?
5. **A** Trying to work out the answers to these philosophy questions is a minefield. ☐
   B Trying to work out the answers to these philosophy questions is a piece of cake.
6. **A** You should go with your gut feeling. ☐
   B You should go with your instinct.

Answer key

1 British and American English words and phrases

Exercise 1
1 elevator
2 cellphone
3 cookie
4 intermission

Exercise 2
1 term
2 underground
3 pavement
4 railway
5 interval
6 biscuits

Exercise 3
1 French fries
2 apartment
3 movie
4 downtown
5 vacation
6 railroad

Exercise 4
1 ground floor
2 city centre
3 post
4 pavement
5 crisps
6 flat

Exercise 5
1 tick
2 autumn
3 cinema
4 chips
5 lift
6 holiday

Exercise 6
1 flat
2 ground floor
3 pavement
4 term
5 bill
6 underground

2 Entertainment and the media

Exercise 1
1 soundtrack, critic
2 bestseller
3 coverage, critic, editor
4 episode
5 lyrics, conductor

Exercise 2
1 Yes
2 Yes
3 No
4 Yes
5 No
6 Yes

Exercise 3
1 cast
2 episodes
3 lyrics
4 applause
5 conductor
6 composer

Exercise 4
1 applause ✓
2 episode ✗
3 cast ✓
4 composed ✗
5 setting ✓
6 soundtrack ✗

Exercise 5
1 costume
2 setting
3 critics
4 plot
5 episodes
6 artistic

3 Places and buildings

Exercise 1
1 b 2 a 3 e 4 f 5 c 6 d

Exercise 2
1 a bistro
2 hammer and nails
3 a landmark.
4 many homes.
5 students can stay cheaply.

Exercise 3
1 industrial estate
2 seaside resort
3 skyline
4 landmark
5 location
6 cashpoint

Exercise 4
1 location
2 house
3 carriageway
4 outskirts
5 ᵃsuburbs, ᵇresidential
6 skyline

Exercise 5
1 Yes
2 No
3 No
4 Yes
5 No
6 Yes
7 Yes

4 Relationships

Exercise 1
1 circle
2 proposal
3 upbringing
4 ancestor
5 widow
6 stepmother

Exercise 2
1 f
2 a
3 d
4 e
5 c
6 b

Exercise 3
1 a
2 e
3 b
4 d
5 f
6 c

Exercise 4
1 fancy
2 propose
3 break
4 stand
5 stick
6 cheating

5 Beliefs and ideas

Exercise 1
1 superstition ✗
2 tolerant ✗
3 philosophy ✓
4 theology ✓
5 open-minded ✗
6 religious ✓

Answer key Units 1–8

Exercise 2
1 civilization   3 myth   5 belief
2 morals   4 ritual   6 philosophy

Exercise 3
1 a   2 e   3 c   4 d   5 b   6 f

Exercise 4
1 No   3 No   5 Yes
2 Yes   4 Yes

Exercise 5
1 religious   3 civilization   5 Theology
2 philosophy   4 nurture   6 superstition

6 Social and political issues

Exercise 1
1 f   2 d   3 a   4 e   5 b   6 c

Exercise 2
1 benefit   3 democracy   5 community
2 poverty   4 nationality   6 consumerism

Exercise 3
1 No   3 No   5 No
2 Yes   4 Yes   6 Yes

Exercise 4
1 'Lifestyle' ✗   5 economics ✗
2 multicultural ✗   6 national ✓
3 welfare ✓   7 contributing ✓
4 Parliament ✓

Exercise 5
1 wealth   3 citizens   5 democracy
2 Consumers   4 council   6 refugees

7 Experiences

Exercise 1
1 c   2 b   3 a   4 f   5 d   6 e

Exercise 2
1 welcoming   4 ᵃskills, ᵇadapted
2 relevant   5 explored
3 ᵃidentity, ᵇworthwhile   6 ᵃstrengths, ᵇweaknesses

Exercise 3
1 I love my new job and feel accepted by the whole team.
2 David has always wanted to be promoted at work, but it is such a small office that there are no real opportunities there.
3 Journalists don't often reveal the identity of their sources.
4 Sarah is very talented. She is an excellent musician.
5 It's not worthwhile learning all this geography. It's won't be useful in my future career.
6 The point you are making is not relevant to this discussion, I'm afraid.

Exercise 4
1 influenced   3 challenge   5 weaknesses
2 adapt   4 accepted   6 used to

Exercise 5
1 upbringing.
2 of value, good to do or to have.
3 Cambridge is where they were born and where they grew up.
4 you are given a higher position, usually with a better salary.
5 the things they do well and the things they need to learn to do better.

8 News and current affairs

Exercise 1
1 column   5 headlines
2 ᵃpress, ᵇdeadline   6 exclusive
3 sources   7 leader
4 mass media

Exercise 2
1 the story has become really important.
2 an official statement from someone about a topic of interest.
3 the news story is available in only one newspaper.
4 current affairs.
5 mass media.
6 a press conference.

Exercise 3
1 press   4 sources
2 leader   5 circulation
3 critic

Exercise 4
1 editorial   4 edit
2 deadline   5 coverage
3 publicity   6 column

Exercise 5
1 No   4 No
2 Yes   5 No
3 Yes   6 Yes

Exercise 6
1 c   2 b   3 d   4 e   5 a   6 f

115

9 The natural world

Exercise 1
1 an active
2 out
3 fertile
4 an endangered
5 rural
6 an ecological

Exercise 2
1 f   2 e   3 b   4 c   5 a   6 d

Exercise 3
1 harvests
2 reserve
3 roots
4 carbon footprint
5 climate change
6 carbon monoxide

Exercise 4
1 volcano
2 evolution
3 global warming
4 rainbow
5 tornado
6 carbon footprint

Exercise 5
1 rural
2 climate change
3 harvests
4 species
5 seed
6 conservation

10 Natural phenomena

Exercise 1
1 blizzard
2 bystander
3 catastrophe
4 famine
5 glacier
6 heatwave

Exercise 2
1 demolishing
2 search dogs
3 trapped
4 survivors
5 shield
6 debris

Exercise 3
1 submerged
2 eruption
3 demolished
4 cut off
5 dug
6 victims

Exercise 4
1 b   2 e   3 a   4 f   5 d   6 c

Exercise 5
1 blizzard
2 eruption
3 catastrophe
4 debris
5 glacier
6 famine

11 House and home

Exercise 1
1 atmosphere
2 houseboat
3 domestic
4 storey
5 settle
6 resident

Exercise 2
1 studio
2 atmosphere
3 domestic
4 storey
5 construction
6 residents

Exercise 3
1 pull down
2 terraced
3 settled in
4 put up
5 hook
6 cabinet

Exercise 4
1 f   2 a   3 d   4 c   5 e   6 b

Exercise 5
1 atmosphere
2 domestic
3 storey
4 construction
5 detached
6 resident

Exercise 6
1 d   2 a   3 f   4 e   5 c   6 b

12 Health, medicine and exercise

Exercise 1
1 blood pressure
2 cholesterol level
3 prescriptions
4 antibiotics
5 wounds
6 surgery

Exercise 2
1 allergy
2 bruise
3 cholesterol level
4 dose
5 plaster
6 surgeon

Exercise 3
1 Yes   3 No   5 Yes
2 No   4 No   6 Yes

Exercise 4
1 antibiotics ✓
2 blood pressure ✓
3 bruise ✗
4 surgery ✓
5 prescription ✗
6 plaster ✗

Exercise 5
1 allergy ✗
2 antibiotics ✓
3 surgery ✓
4 doses ✗
5 runny noses ✗
6 rash ✗

13 Feelings

Exercise 1
1 pessimistic
2 aggressive
3 determined
4 guilty
5 helpless
6 hurt

Exercise 2
1 c   3 e   5 f
2 b   4 d   6 a

116   **Work on your Vocabulary** Upper Intermediate (B2)

Answer key Units 9–17

Exercise 3
1 No 3 Yes 5 No
2 Yes 4 No

Exercise 4
1 sociable 3 puzzled 5 aggressive
2 suspicious 4 frustration 6 upset

Exercise 5
1 disgusting ✓ 4 determined ✗
2 fair ✗ 5 sociable ✓
3 upset ✓ 6 puzzled ✗

14 Music and the arts

Exercise 1
1 abstract 3 exhibition 5 model
2 portrait 4 landscape

Exercise 2
1 model 4 track 7 conductor
2 gig 5 backing group
3 melody 6 portrait

Exercise 3
1 music 3 gig 5 model
2 chorus 4 abstract

Exercise 4
1 conductor 4 guitarist
2 soloist 5 ªmelody, ᵇlyrics
3 rhythm 6 backing

Exercise 5
1 vocalist 3 landscape 5 rhythm
2 tracks 4 exhibition 6 music

Exercise 6
1 music 4 soloist 7 kit
2 conductor 5 melody
3 beat 6 guitarist

15 Crime and law

Exercise 1
1 arrested 4 innocence
2 charged 5 committed a crime
3 burglary 6 judge

Exercise 2
1 court 5 finding
2 charged 6 judge
3 innocent 7 punishment
4 witnesses

Exercise 3
1 witness 3 justice 5 criminal
2 jury 4 burglary 6 judge

Exercise 4
1 charged 3 trial 5 found
2 illegal 4 witnesses 6 innocence

Exercise 5
1 let off 4 break the law
2 punishment 5 committed a crime
3 defend 6 jury

Exercise 6
1 No 3 Yes 5 No
2 Yes 4 Yes 6 Yes

16 Communication

Exercise 1
1 a 2 d 3 f 4 b 5 c 6 e

Exercise 2
1 emphasize 4 smartphone
2 fluency 5 account
3 quarrelled 6 summed up

Exercise 3
1 highlight 3 update 5 draft
2 misleading 4 chart 6 interact

Exercise 4
1 draft 3 boasts 5 clear
2 charts 4 tone 6 misleading

Exercise 5
1 brought ✗ 4 underline ✓
2 delivering ✓ 5 update ✓
3 speak ✗ 6 quarrelling ✗

17 Words and phrases for linking ideas

Exercise 1
1 Yes 3 Yes 5 No
2 No 4 Yes 6 Yes

Exercise 2
1 even if 4 besides
2 With reference to 5 Just as
3 at any rate

Exercise 3
1 That is to say ✓ 4 to conclude ✓
2 even so ✗ 5 as ✗
3 On the contrary ✓ 6 furthermore ✓

117

Exercise 4
1 In the first place
2 Not only
3 In other words
4 What is more
5 Even though
6 To conclude

Exercise 5
1 No
2 Yes
3 No
4 No
5 Yes

Exercise 6
1 follows
2 even though
3 In other words
4 at any rate

18 Work and jobs

Exercise 1
1 incomes
2 candidate
3 appoint
4 commerce
5 skilled
6 flexi-time

Exercise 2
1 consultant
2 duties
3 overtime
4 provide
5 incomes
6 strike

Exercise 3
1 Yes
2 No
3 No
4 Yes
5 Yes
6 No

Exercise 4
1 a 2 e 3 b 4 f 5 d 6 c

19 Travel and holidays

Exercise 1
1 b 2 c 3 e 4 f 5 d 6 a

Exercise 2
1 get away
2 scheduled
3 landed
4 immigration
5 terminal
6 stopover

Exercise 3
1 pulled out
2 go on
3 pulled over
4 connection
5 stuck
6 turn up

Exercise 4
1 lanes
2 your connection
3 flight
4 goods
5 a boat
6 transport

Exercise 5
1 parachute
2 aircraft
3 trekking
4 terminal
5 immigration
6 connection

Exercise 6
1 up ✓
2 past ✗
3 onto ✗
4 up ✓
5 off ✗
6 form ✓

20 Prefixes and suffixes

Exercise 1
1 dishonest
2 energetic
3 offensive
4 unbearable
5 harmless
6 misleading

Exercise 2
1 harmless
2 cooperative
3 faithful
4 illegal
5 Loneliness

Exercise 3
1 cares about how other people are feeling.
2 works extra hours in their job.
3 useful every day.
4 raincoats.
5 it looks like the real model.

Exercise 4
1 e 2 f 3 a 4 d 5 b 6 c

Exercise 5
1 offensive
2 disorganized
3 lifelike
4 overtime
5 waterproof
6 irregular

Exercise 6
1 harmless
2 lifelike
3 cooperative
4 loneliness
5 misleading
6 sympathetic

21 Register – formal vs. informal

Exercise 1
1 persons
2 residing
3 commencing
4 offspring
5 ensuring
6 residence

Exercise 2
1 d 3 g 5 c 7 h
2 a 4 e 6 f 8 b

Exercise 3
1 plus
2 buddies
3 bloke
4 shades
5 quid
6 the box

Exercise 4
1 afterwards
2 cop
3 brolly
4 start
5 shades
6 children

22 Words that are used together (collocations)

Exercise 1
1 d 3 c 5 e
2 f 4 b 6 a

Answer key Units 18–26

Exercise 2
1 keep 3 caught 5 heavy
2 make 4 changed 6 take

Exercise 3
1 sight 3 point 5 start
2 second 4 crime 6 experience

Exercise 4
1 make 3 keep 5 give
2 steady 4 meet 6 change

Exercise 5
1 I caught sight of Amir in the crowd.
2 That majestic old tree has caught fire.
3 I can't tell the difference between these wines.
4 Jack hardly makes a living from his work.
5 The traffic was so heavy that we were late.
6 Hannah wants to raise her family in the countryside.

23 Education

Exercise 1
1 e 2 f 3 a 4 b 5 d 6 c

Exercise 2
1 credit 4 graduate
2 seminar 5 certificate
3 slide 6 further education

Exercise 3
1 certificate, slide 3 specialize, admission
2 campus, tutorial 4 theses, credits

Exercise 4
1 dissertation, assignment
2 workshop, seminar
3 tutor, graduate

Exercise 5
1 Yes 3 No 5 No
2 No 4 Yes 6 Yes

Exercise 6
1 slides 3 thesis 5 specializes
2 tutorial 4 admission 6 qualifies

24 Information technology

Exercise 1
1 database 4 bookmarks
2 application 5 broadband
3 attachment 6 virtual reality

Exercise 2
1 back up 3 charge 5 log in 7 run
2 browse 4 crashes 6 store 8 burn

Exercise 3
1 d 2 e 3 c 4 a 5 b 6 f

Exercise 4
1 She performed an experiment to prove her theory.
2 An interactive tutorial teaches you the basics of the software.
3 Double-click on the program icon to run it.
4 I need a special cable to connect my phone to my computer.
5 Check that there are no loose wires.
6 Is there a socket where I can plug this in?

25 Services

Exercise 1
1 private ward 3 hospitality. 5 room service
2 a paramedic 4 a safe

Exercise 2
1 GP surgery
2 compulsory education
3 consultant
4 tourist trail
5 natural history museum
6 standards

Exercise 3
1 paramedic 4 private healthcare
2 GP surgery 5 facilities
3 consultant 6 outpatients

Exercise 4
1 customer service 4 convenience
2 food outlet 5 facilities
3 deposit 6 outpatient

Exercise 5
1 Yes 3 Yes 5 Yes
2 No 4 No 6 No

26 People

Exercise 1
1 adventurous 3 responsible 5 pale
2 enthusiastic 4 astonished 6 admire

Exercise 2
1 ambitious 3 amused 5 well-built
2 cautious 4 generous 6 plump

Exercise 3
1 d 2 f 3 a 4 c 5 b 6 e

Exercise 4
1 Yes 3 Yes 5 No
2 No 4 Yes

Exercise 5
1 wavy 3 generous 5 astonished
2 plump 4 amused 6 bright

Exercise 6
1 ambitious 4 generous
2 cautious 5 adventurous
3 admired 6 enthusiastic

27 Seeing, hearing, touching, smelling and tasting

Exercise 1
1 stare ✗ 3 flavourful ✗ 5 rotten ✓
2 deafening ✓ 4 fluffy ✓ 6 stinking ✗

Exercise 2
1 whisper 3 stinks
2 yell 4 spectators

Exercise 3
1 witness 3 monotonous 5 scanned
2 stare 4 sip 6 scented

Exercise 4
1 sharp 2 fluffy 3 sip

Exercise 5
1 overheard 3 sharp 5 flavour
2 grabbed 4 scanned

28 Movement and speed

Exercise 1
1 d 2 c 3 f 4 a 5 b 6 e

Exercise 2
1 Yes 3 Yes 5 No
2 No 4 No 6 Yes

Exercise 3
1 dash 3 sound 5 hike
2 race 4 hurry 6 stroll

Exercise 4
1 get 3 stroll 5 rush
2 fly 4 sound 6 moved into

Exercise 5
1 noise ✗ 3 away ✓ 5 trek ✓
2 out ✗ 4 stroll ✓ 6 marched ✗

29 Phrases with be, do, get, have and make

Exercise 1
1 make matters worse 4 make up for
2 make sense 5 make fun of
3 make a profit 6 make up

Exercise 2
1 Yes 3 Yes 5 Yes
2 No 4 No

Exercise 3
1 doing it up
2 doesn't make sense *or* makes no sense
3 made into
4 does harm

Exercise 4
1 c 2 b 3 d 4 a 5 e

Exercise 5
1 Yes 3 No 5 No
2 Yes 4 Yes 6 Yes

Exercise 6
1 made a fool of herself ✓ 4 make the most of it ✓
2 makes matters bad ✗ 5 made it out ✗
3 makes sense ✓ 6 makes up ✗

30 Metaphorical language

Exercise 1
1 a 2 d 3 c 4 e 5 f 6 b

Exercise 2
1 turn 3 planted 5 drags
2 leaked 4 water 6 gut

Exercise 3
1 rules 3 a wish 5 savings
2 by hand 4 anger 6 a comparison

Exercise 4
1 Yes 3 Yes 5 No
2 No 4 No 6 Yes

Exercise 5
1 burden 3 gut 5 minefield
2 bury 4 crossed 6 fiery

Exercise 6
1 No 3 No 5 No
2 Yes 4 Yes 6 Yes

Pronunciation guide

We have used the International Phonetic Alphabet (IPA) to show how the words are pronounced.

IPA Symbols

Vowel sounds

ɑː	calm, ah
æ	act, mass
aɪ	dive, cry
aɪə	fire, tyre
aʊ	out, down
aʊə	flour, sour
e	met, lend, pen
eɪ	say, weight
eə	fair, care
ɪ	fit, win
iː	seem, me
ɪə	near, beard
ɒ	lot, spot
əʊ	note, coat
ɔː	claw, more
ɔɪ	boy, joint
ʊ	could, stood
uː	you, use
ʊə	sure, pure
ɜː	turn, third
ʌ	fund, must
ə	the first vowel in about

Consonant Sounds

b	bed, rub
d	done, red
f	fit, if
g	good, dog
h	hat, horse
j	yellow, you
k	king, pick
l	lip, bill
m	mat, ram
n	not, tin
p	pay, lip
r	run, read
s	soon, bus
t	talk, bet
v	van, love
w	win, wool
x	loch
z	zoo, buzz
ʃ	ship, wish
ʒ	measure, leisure
ŋ	sing, working
tʃ	cheap, witch
θ	thin, myth
ð	then, bathe
dʒ	joy, bridge

Notes

Primary and secondary stress are shown by marks above and below the line, in front of the stressed syllable. For example, in the word abbreviation, /əˌbriːviˈeɪʃən/, the second syllable has secondary stress and the fourth syllable has primary stress.

Index

The numbers refer to the unit numbers, not page numbers.

A

abstract /ˈæbstrækt/ 14
academic /ˌækəˈdemɪk/ 23
accepted /əkˈseptɪd/ 7
account /əˈkaʊnt/ 16, 25
adapt to /əˈdæpt tuː, AM tə/ 7
addicted /əˈdɪktɪd/ 26
admire /ədˈmaɪə/ 26
admission /ædˈmɪʃən/ 23
adoption /əˈdɒpʃən/ 4
advantage /ædˈvɑːntɪdʒ, AM-ˈvæn-/ 21, 25
adventurous /ædˈventʃərəs/ 26
affairs /əˈfeəz/ 8
after all /ˌɑːftəˈɔːl, AM ˌæftə/ 17
afterwards /ˈɑːftəwədz, AM ˈæf-/ 21
aggressive /əˈɡresɪv/ 13, 26
AIDS /eɪdz/ 12
aircraft /ˈeəkrɑːft, AM-kræft/ 19
allergy /ˈælədʒi/ 12
ambitious /æmˈbɪʃəs/ 26
amused /əˈmjuːzd/ 26
ancestor /ˈænsestə/ 4
antibiotics /ˌæntibaɪˈɒtɪks/ 12
apartment /əˈpɑːtmənt/ 1
applause /əˈplɔːz/ 2
application /ˌæplɪˈkeɪʃən/ 24
appoint /əˈpɔɪnt/ 18
appreciate /əˈpriːʃieɪt/ 26
area /ˈeəriə/ 3
arrest /əˈrest/ 15
artistic /ɑːˈtɪstɪk/ 2
as a consequence /ˌæz əˈkɒnsɪkwəns/ 17
as far as I know /əz ˌfɑːr əzˈaɪ ˌnəʊ/ 5
as follows /ˌæzˈfɒləʊz/ 17
assignment /əˈsaɪnmənt/ 23
astonished /əˈstɒnɪʃt/ 26
at any rate /ætˈeniˌreɪt/ 17
at the same time /æt ðəˌseɪmˈtaɪm/ 17
ATM /ˌeɪ tiːˈem/ 3
atmosphere /ˈætməsfɪə/ 11
attachment /əˈtætʃmənt/ 24
attention /əˈtenʃən/ 16
autumn /ˈɔːtəm/ 1

B

back up /ˈbækˌʌp/ 24
backing group /ˈbækɪŋˌɡruːp/ 14
ballot /ˈbælət/ 6
bank account /ˈbæŋk əˌkaʊnt/ 25
bass guitarist /ˌbeɪs ɡɪˈtɑːrɪst/ 14
bay /beɪ/ 3
be influenced by /biːˈɪnfluənstˌbaɪ/ 7
be to do with something /biː təˈduː wɪð ˈsʌmθɪŋ/ 29
beat /biːt/ 14
begin /bɪˈɡɪn/ 21
belief /bɪˈliːf/ 5
bench /bentʃ/ 11
benefit /ˈbenɪfɪt/ 6
besides /bɪˈsaɪdz/ 17
bestseller /ˌbestˈselə/ 2
bill /bɪl/ 1
biscuit /ˈbɪskɪt/ 1
bistro /ˈbiːstrəʊ/ 3
blackout /ˈblækaʊt/ 30
blizzard /ˈblɪzəd/ 10
block /blɒk/ 11
bloke /bləʊk/ 21
blood pressure /ˈblʌdˌpreʃə/ 12
boast /bəʊst/ 16
bookmark /ˈbʊkmɑːk/ 24
born and bred /ˌbɔːn ændˈbred/ 7
boss /bɒs/ 21
box /bɒks/ 21
break someone's heart /ˌbreɪk ˈsʌmwʌnz ˈhɑːt/ 4
break the law /ˌbreɪk ðəˈlɔː/ 15
bred /bred/ 7
bright /braɪt/ 26
broadband /ˈbrɔːdbænd/ 24
brolly /ˈbrɒli/ 21
brother-in-law /ˈbrʌðərɪnˌlɔː/ 4
browse /braʊz/ 24
bruise /bruːz/ 12

buddy /ˈbʌdi/ 21
bungalow /ˈbʌŋɡələʊ/ 11
burden /ˈbɜːdən/ 30
bureaucracy /bjʊˈrɒkrəsi/ 6
burglar /ˈbɜːɡlə/ 15
burglary /ˈbɜːɡləri/ 15
burn /bɜːn/ 24
bury /ˈberi/ 30
by ear /ˌbaɪˈɪə/ 30
by heart /ˌbaɪˈhɑːt/ 30
bystander /ˈbaɪstændə/ 10

C

cabinet /ˈkæbɪnət/ 11
cable /ˈkeɪbəl/ 24
calm /kɑːm/ 22
campus /ˈkæmpəs/ 23
candidate /ˈkændɪdeɪt/ 18
capture /ˈkæptʃə/ 2
carbon dioxide /ˌkɑːbən daɪˈɒksaɪd/ 9
carbon footprint /ˌkɑːbənˈfʊtprɪnt/ 9
carbon monoxide /ˌkɑːbən məˈnɒksaɪd/ 9
care /keə/ 25
career path /kəˈrɪəˌpɑːθ/ 30
caring /ˈkeərɪŋ/ 26
carriageway /ˈkærɪdʒweɪ/ 3
case /keɪs/ 17
cashpoint /ˈkæʃpɔɪnt/ 3
cast /kɑːst, kæst/ 2
catastrophe /kəˈtæstrəfi/ 10
catch a glimpse /ˌkætʃ əˈɡlɪmps/ 27
catch fire /ˌkætʃˈfaɪə/ 22
catch sight of /ˌkætʃˈsaɪt ɒv, əv/ 22
catch someone's attention /ˌkætʃ ˈsʌmwʌnz əˈtenʃən/ 16
catch someone's eye /ˌkætʃ ˈsʌmwʌnzˈaɪ/ 22
cautious /ˈkɔːʃəs/ 26
celeb /sɪˈleb/ 21
celebrity /sɪˈlebrɪti/ 21
cellphone /ˈselfəʊn/ 1

Work on your Vocabulary Upper Intermediate (B2)

Index

certificate /səˈtɪfɪkət/ 23
challenge /ˈtʃælɪndʒ/ 7
change the subject /ˌtʃeɪndʒ ðə ˈsʌbdʒekt/ 22
change your mind /ˌtʃeɪndʒ jɔːˈmaɪnd, jə/ 5
charge /tʃɑːdʒ/ 15, 24
chart /tʃɑːt/ 16
check /tʃek/ 1
chips /tʃɪps/ 1
cholesterol level /kəˈlestərɒlˌlevəl, AM -rɔːl/ 12
chorus /ˈkɔːrəs/ 14
cinema /ˈsɪnɪmɑː/ 1
circle /ˈsɜːkəl/ 4
circulation /ˌsɜːkjuˈleɪʃən/ 8
citizen /ˈsɪtɪzən/ 6
city centre /ˌsɪtiˈsentə/ 1
civilization /ˌsɪvɪlaɪˈzeɪʃən/ 5
classic /ˈklæsɪk/ 2
clear something up /ˌklɪə sʌmθɪŋˈʌp/ 16
client /ˈklaɪənt/ 18
cliff /klɪf/ 3
climate change /ˈklaɪmətˌtʃeɪndʒ/ 9
collapse /kəˈlæps/ 30
column /ˈkɒləm/ 8
columnist /ˈkɒləmɪst/ 8
come flying /ˌkʌmˈflaɪɪŋ/ 28
come second /ˌkʌmˈsekənd/ 22
come to the point /ˌkʌm tə ðəˈpɔɪnt/ 22
commence /kəˈmens/ 21
commerce /ˈkɒmɜːs/ 18
commit a crime /kəˌmɪt əˈkraɪm/ 15, 22
community /kəˈmjuːnɪti/ 6
competition /ˌkɒmpɪˈtɪʃən/ 18
compose /kəmˈpəʊz/ 2
composer /kəmˈpəʊzə/ 2
compulsory education /kəmˌpʌlsəriˌedʒuˈkeɪʃən/ 25
conclude /kənˈkluːd/ 17
conductor /kənˈdʌktə/ 2, 14
conference /ˈkɒnfrəns/ 8
connection /kəˈnekʃən/ 19
consequence /ˈkɒnsɪkwəns/ 17
consequently /ˈkɒnsɪkwəntli/ 21
conservation /ˌkɒnsəˈveɪʃən/ 9
construction /kənˈstrʌkʃən/ 11
consultant /kənˈsʌltənt/ 18, 25
consumer /kənˈsjuːmə, AM -ˈsuː-/ 6

consumerism /kənˈsjuːmərɪzəm, AM -ˈsuː-/ 6
contradict /ˌkɒntrəˈdɪkt/ 21
contrary /ˈkɒntrəri, AM -treri/ 17
contribute /kənˈtrɪbjuːt/ 6
convenience /kənˈviːniəns/ 25
convinced /kənˈvɪnst/ 5
cookie /ˈkuki/ 1
cooperative /kəʊˈɒpərətɪv/ 20
cop /kɒp/ 21
costume /ˈkɒstjuːm, AM -tuːm/ 2
council /ˈkaunsəl/ 6
councillor /ˈkaunsələ/ 6
court /kɔːt/ 15
coverage /ˈkʌvərɪdʒ/ 2, 8
coward /kauəd/ 26
crash /kræʃ/ 24
credible /ˈkredɪbəl/ 5
credit /ˈkredɪt/ 23
crew /kruː/ 18
crime /kraɪm/ 15, 22
criminal /ˈkrɪmɪnəl/ 15
crisps /krɪsps/ 1
critic /ˈkrɪtɪk/ 2, 8
cross your mind /ˌkrɒs jɔːˈmaɪnd, jə/ 30
current affairs /ˌkʌrənt əˈfeəz/ 8
customer service /ˌkʌstəməˈsɜːvɪs/ 25
cut off /ˌkʌtˈɒf/ 10

D

dash /dæʃ/ 28
database /ˈdeɪtəˌbeɪs/ 24
deadline /ˈdedlaɪn/ 8, 18, 22
deafening /ˈdefənɪŋ/ 27
deal /diːl/ 18
debate /dɪˈbeɪt/ 23
debris /ˈdeɪbri, AM deɪˈbriː/ 10
deck /dek/ 19
defend /dɪˈfend/ 15
deliver a speech /dɪˌlɪvər əˈspiːtʃ/ 16
democracy /dɪˈmɒkrəsi/ 6
demolish /dɪˈmɒlɪʃ/ 10
demonstrate /ˈdemənstreɪt/ 21
deposit /dɪˈpɒzɪt/ 25
detached /dɪˈtætʃt/ 11
determined /dɪˈtɜːmɪnd/ 13
difference /ˈdɪfrəns/ 22
dig /dɪg/ 10
dig up /ˌdɪgˈʌp/ 30
dioxide /daɪˈɒksaɪd/ 9

disbelieve /ˌdɪsbɪˈliːv/ 5
disgusting /dɪsˈgʌstɪŋ/ 13
dishonest /dɪsˈɒnɪst/ 20
disorganized /dɪsˈɔːgənaɪzd/ 20
dissertation /ˌdɪsəˈteɪʃən/ 23
do /duː/ 29
do an exam /ˌduː ən ɪgˈzæm/ 23
do damage /ˌduːˈdæmɪdʒ/ 29
do harm /ˌduːˈhɑːm/ 29
do someone good /ˌduː sʌmwʌnˈgʊd/ 29
do up /ˌduːˈʌp/ 29
do without /ˌduː wɪðˈaʊt/ 29
dog /dɒg, AM dɔːg/ 10
domestic /dəˈmestɪk/ 11
dose /dəʊs/ 12
downtown /ˈdaʊntaʊn/ 1
draft /drɑːft, AM dræft/ 16
drag /dræg/ 30
drops /drɒps/ 12
drum kit /ˈdrʌmˌkɪt/ 14
dual carriageway /ˌdjuːəlˈkærɪdʒweɪ, AMˈduːəl/ 3
duty /ˈdjuːti, AMˈduːti/ 18

E

ear /ɪə/ 30
ecological /ˌiːkəˈlɒdʒɪkəl/ 9
economics /ˌiːkəˈnɒmɪks, AM ˌek-/ 6
economy /ɪˈkɒnəmi/ 6
edit /ˈedɪt/ 8
editor /ˈedɪtə/ 2, 8
editorial /ˌedɪˈtɔːriəl/ 8
education /ˌedʒuˈkeɪʃən/ 23, 25
elevator /ˈelɪveɪtə/ 1
emphasize /ˈemfəsaɪz/ 16
endangered /ɪnˈdeɪndʒəd/ 9
energetic /ˌenəˈdʒetɪk/ 20
ensure /ɪnˈʃʊə/ 21
entertaining /ˌentəˈteɪnɪŋ/ 2
enthusiastic /ɪnˌθjuːziˈæstɪk, AM -ˌθuː-/ 26
episode /ˈepɪsəʊd/ 2
eruption /ɪˈrʌpʃən/ 10
establish /ɪˈstæblɪʃ/ 18
estate /ɪˈsteɪt/ 3
evacuation /ɪˌvækjuˈeɪʃən/ 10
even if /ˈiːvənˌɪf/ 17
even so /ˌiːvənˈsəʊ/ 17
evolution /ˌiːvəˈluːʃən, AM ev-/ 9
exclusive /ɪkˈskluːsɪv/ 8
exhausted /ɪgˈzɔːstɪd/ 13
exhibit /ɪgˈzɪbɪt/ 14

exhibition /ˌeksɪˈbɪʃən/ 14
experience /ɪkˈspɪəriəns/ 7, 22
experiment /ɪkˈsperɪmənt/ 24
explore /ɪkˈsplɔː/ 7
eye /aɪ/ 22
eye drops /ˈaɪˌdrɒps/ 12

F

facilities /fəˈsɪlɪtiːz/ 25
fair /feə/ 13
faithful /ˈfeɪθful/ 4, 20
fall /fɔːl/ 1
family /ˈfæmɪli/ 22
famine /ˈfæmɪn/ 10
fancy /ˈfænsi/ 4
far /fɑː/ 5
feature /ˈfiːtʃə/ 8, 26
feel accepted /ˌfiːl əkˈseptɪd/ 7
fiery /ˈfaɪəri/ 30
film /fɪlm/ 1
find someone guilty /ˌfaɪnd sʌmwʌnˈgɪlti/ 15
find someone not guilty /ˌfaɪnd sʌmwʌnˈnɒtˌgɪlti/ 15
fire /faɪə/ 22
first floor /ˌfɜːstˈflɔː/ 1
flat /flæt/ 1
flavour /ˈfleɪvə/ 27
flavourful /ˈfleɪvəful/ 27
flavourless /ˈfleɪvələs/ 27
flexi-time /ˈfleksiˌtaɪm/ 18
fluency /ˈfluːənsi/ 16
fluffy /ˈflʌfi/ 27
flying /ˈflaɪɪŋ/ 28
follows /ˈfɒləʊz/ 17
food outlet /ˈfuːdˌaʊtlet/ 25
fool /fuːl/ 29
footprint /ˈfʊtprɪnt/ 9
French Fries /ˌfrentʃˈfraɪz/ 1
fresh start /ˌfreʃˈstɑːt/ 22
friend /frend/ 21
fries /fraɪz/ 1
frustration /frʌˈstreɪʃən/ 13
fun /fʌn/ 29
functional /ˈfʌŋkʃənəl/ 20
funeral /ˈfjuːnərəl/ 4
further education /ˌfɜːðər edʒuˈkeɪʃən/ 23
furthermore /ˌfɜːðəˈmɔː/ 17

G

gain experience /ˌgeɪn ɪkˈspɪəriəns/ 7, 22

generous /ˈdʒenərəs/ 26
get away /ˌget əˈweɪ/ 19
get moving /ˌgetˈmuːvɪŋ/ 28
get something across /ˌget sʌmθɪŋ əˈkrɒs/ 16
get used to /ˌgetˈjuːst tuː, AM tə/ 7, 29
gig /gɪg/ 14
give a presentation /ˌgɪv əˌprezənˈteɪʃən, AMˌpriːzen-/ 22
glacier /ˈglæsiə, AMˈgleɪʃə/ 10
glance /glɑːns, AM glæns/ 27
glimpse /glɪmps/ 27
global warming /ˌgləʊbəlˈwɔːmɪŋ/ 9
go against /ˌgəʊ əˈgenst/ 21
go flying /ˌgəʊˈflaɪɪŋ/ 28
go to press /ˌgəʊ təˈpres/ 8
govern /ˈgʌvən/ 6
government /ˈgʌvənmənt/ 6
GP surgery /ˌdʒiːˌpiːˈsɜːdʒəri/ 25
grab /græb/ 27
graduate /(noun)ˈgrædʒuːət; (verb)ˈgrædʒueɪt/ 23
graduate from /ˈgrædʒueɪt frɒm, frəm/ 7, 23
ground floor /ˌgraʊndˈflɔː/ 1
group /gruːp/ 14
guilty /ˈgɪlti/ 13
guitarist /gɪˈtɑːrɪst/ 14
gut feeling /ˌgʌtˈfiːlɪŋ/ 30
guy /gaɪ/ 21

H

hardware store /ˈhɑːdweəˌstɔː/ 3
harm /hɑːm/ 29
harmless /ˈhɑːmləs/ 20
harvest /ˈhɑːvɪst/ 9
have a word with someone /ˌhæv əˈwɜːd wɪð sʌmwʌn/ 16
have to do with something /ˌhæv təˈduː wɪð sʌmθɪŋ/ 29
headlines /ˈhedlaɪnz/ 8
healthcare /ˈhelθkeə/ 25
heart /hɑːt/ 4, 30
heatwave /ˈhiːtˌweɪv/ 10
heavy traffic /ˌheviˈtræfɪk/ 22
helpless /ˈhelpləs/ 13
highlight /ˈhaɪlaɪt/ 16
high-rise /ˈhaɪraɪz/ 11
hike /haɪk/ 28

hit the headlines /ˌhɪt ðəˈhedlaɪnz/ 8
holiday /ˈhɒlɪdeɪ/ 1
home /həʊm/ 21
hook /hʊk/ 11
horizon /həˈraɪzən/ 3
horn /hɔːn/ 19
horrified /ˈhɒrɪfaɪd, AMˈhɔːr-/ 13
hospitality /ˌhɒspɪˈtælɪti/ 25
hostel /ˈhɒstəl/ 3
hour /aʊə/ 19
house /haʊs/ 11
houseboat /ˈhaʊsbəʊt/ 11
hurry /ˈhʌri, AMˈhɜːri/ 28
hurt /hɜːt/ 13

I

identity /aɪˈdentɪti/ 7
illegal /ɪˈliːgəl/ 15, 20
illegally /ɪˈliːgəli/ 15
immigration /ˌɪmɪˈgreɪʃən/ 19
impolite /ˌɪmpəˈlaɪt/ 20
in a hurry /ɪn əˈhʌri/ 28
in any case /ɪnˈeniˌkeɪs/ 17
in other words /ɪnˈʌðəˌwɜːdz/ 17
in the first place /ɪn ðəˈfɜːstˌpleɪs/ 17
income /ˈɪnkʌm/ 18, 22
industrial estate /ɪnˈdʌstriəl ɪˌsteɪt/ 3
influenced /ˈɪnfluənst/ 7
injection /ɪnˈdʒekʃən/ 12
innocence /ˈɪnəsəns/ 15
innocent /ˈɪnəsənt/ 15
innocently /ˈɪnəsəntli/ 15
interact /ˌɪntəˈrækt/ 16
interactive /ˌɪntəˈræktɪv/ 24
intermission /ˌɪntəˈmɪʃən/ 1
interval /ˈɪntəvəl/ 1
irregular /ɪˈregjulə/ 20
issue /ˈɪsjuː, ˈɪʃuː/ 21

J

jam /dʒæm/ 19
judge /dʒʌdʒ/ 15
jury /ˈdʒʊəri/ 15
just as ... so /ˌdʒʌst æz ...ˈsəʊ, AM əz/ 17
justice /ˈdʒʌstɪs/ 15

K

keep a promise /ˌkiːp əˈprɒmɪs/ 22

Index

keep calm /ˌkiːpˈkɑːm/ 22
keep your head above water /ˌkiːp jəˌhed əˈbʌvˈwɔːtə, ɔː/ 30
keep your speed up /ˌkiːp jɔːˈspiːd ʌp, AM jə/ 28
kids /kɪdz/ 21
kit /kɪt/ 14
know /nəʊ/ 5

L

land /lænd/ 19
landmark /ˈlændmɑːk/ 3
landscape /ˈlændskeɪp/ 14
lane /leɪn/ 19
later /ˈleɪtə/ 21
law /lɔː/ 15
lead guitarist /ˌliːd gɪˈtɑːrɪst/ 14
leader /ˈliːdə/ 7, 8
leak /liːk/ 30
legal /ˈliːgəl/ 15
legally /ˈliːgəli/ 15
legend /ˈledʒənd/ 5
let someone off /ˌlet sʌmwʌnˈɒf/ 15
level /ˈlevəl/ 12
lifelike /ˈlaɪflaɪk/ 20
lifestyle /ˈlaɪfstaɪl/ 6
lift /lɪft/ 1
lift your spirits /lɪft jɔːˈspɪrɪts, AM jə/ 30
live /laɪv/ 21
living /ˈlɪvɪŋ/ 22
location /ləʊˈkeɪʃən/ 3
log in /ˌlɒgˈɪn/ 24
log off/out /ˌlɒgˈɒf/ˈaʊt/ 24
loneliness /ˈləʊnlinəs/ 20
lonely /ˈləʊnli/ 13
loss /lɒs, AM lɔːs/ 29
lyrics /ˈlɪrɪks/ 2, 14

M

mail /meɪl/ 1
maintain /meɪnˈteɪn/ 5
make /meɪk/ 29
make a fool (out) of yourself /ˌmeɪk əˈfuːl (aʊt) əv jɔːˈself/ 29
make a living /ˌmeɪk əˈlɪvɪŋ/ 22
make a loss /ˌmeɪk əˈlɒs/ 29
make a profit /ˌmeɪk əˈprɒfɪt/ 22, 29
make for /ˈmeɪk fɔː, AM fə/ 29

make fun of /ˌmeɪkˈfʌn ɒv, AM əv/ 29
make into /ˈmeɪkˌɪntuː, AM ɪntə/ 29
make out /ˌmeɪkˈaʊt/ 29
make sense /ˌmeɪkˈsens/ 29
make sure /ˌmeɪkˈʃʊə/ 21
make the best of /ˌmeɪk ðəˈbest ɒv, AM əv/ 29
make the most /ˌmeɪk ðəˈməʊst ɒv, AM əv/ 29
make up /ˌmeɪkˈʌp/ 29
make up for /ˌmeɪkˈʌp fɔː, AM fə/ 29
man /mæn/ 21
manager /ˈmænɪdʒə/ 21
march /mɑːtʃ/ 28
mask /mɑːsk, AM mæsk/ 30
mass media /ˌmæsˈmiːdɪə/ 8
mate /meɪt/ 21
matters /ˈmætəz/ 29
media /ˈmiːdɪə/ 8
meet a deadline /ˌmiːt əˈdedlaɪn/ 22
melody /ˈmelədi/ 14
mind /maɪnd/ 5, 30
minefield /ˈmaɪnfiːld/ 30
miserable /ˈmɪzərəbəl/ 13
misleading /ˌmɪsˈliːdɪŋ/ 16, 20
mobile /ˈməʊbaɪl/ 1
mobile phone /ˌməʊbaɪlˈfəʊn/ 1
model /ˈmɒdəl/ 14
monotonous /məˈnɒtənəs/ 27
monoxide /məˈnɒksaɪd/ 9
moral /ˈmɒrəl, AMˈmɔːr-/ 5
more /mɔː/ 17
movable /ˈmuːvəbəl/ 28
move away /ˌmuːv əˈweɪ/ 28
move into /ˌmuːvˈɪntuː/ 28
move out of /ˌmuːvˈaʊt ɒv, AM əv/ 28
movement /ˈmuːvmənt/ 28
movie /ˈmuːvi/ 1
movie theater /ˈmuːviˌθiːətə/ 1
multicultural /ˌmʌltiˈkʌltʃərəl/ 6
multistorey /ˌmʌltiˈstɔːri/ 3
museum /mjuːˈziːəm/ 25
music /ˈmjuːzɪk/ 14
myth /mɪθ/ 5

N

narrow-minded /ˌnærəʊˈmaɪndɪd/ 5
nation /ˈneɪʃən/ 6

national /ˈnæʃənəl/ 6
nationality /ˌnæʃəˈnælɪti/ 6
natural history museum /ˌnætʃərəlˈhɪstəri mjuːˌziːəm/ 25
nevertheless /ˌnevəðəˈles/ 17
nose /nəʊz/ 12
not only ... but also /nɒtˈəʊnli ... bʌtˈɔːlsəʊ/ 17
nurture /ˈnɜːtʃə/ 5

O

of course /əvˈkɔːs/ 17
offensive /əˈfensɪv/ 20
offspring /ˈɒfsprɪŋ, AMˈɔːf-/ 21
on the contrary /ˌɒn ðəˈcɒntrəri/ 17
one-way street /ˌwʌnweɪˈstriːt/ 3
open-minded /ˌəʊpənˈmaɪndɪd/ 5
opera house /ˈɒpərəˌhaʊs/ 3
optimistic /ˌɒptɪˈmɪstɪk/ 13
outpatient /ˈaʊtpeɪʃənt/ 25
outskirts /ˈaʊtskɜːts/ 3
overhear /ˌəʊvəˈhɪə/ 27
overtake /ˌəʊvəˈteɪk/ 19
overtime /ˈəʊvətaɪm/ 18, 20

P

painkiller /ˈpeɪnˌkɪlə/ 12
pal /pæl/ 21
pale /peɪl/ 26
parachute /ˈpærəʃuːt/ 19
paramedic /ˌpærəˈmedɪk, AM -medɪk/ 25
parliament /ˈpɑːləmənt/ 6
path /pɑːθ, AM pæθ/ 30
pavement /ˈpeɪvmənt/ 1
people /ˈpiːpəl/ 21
persons /ˈpɜːsənz/ 21
pessimistic /ˌpesɪˈmɪstɪk/ 13
philosophy /fɪˈlɒsəfi/ 5
phone /fəʊn/ 1, 16
place /pleɪs/ 17, 21
plant /plɑːnt, AM plænt/ 30
plaster /ˈplɑːstə, AMˈplæstə/ 12
plot /plɒt/ 2
plug /plʌg/ 24
plump /plʌmp/ 26
plus /plʌs/ 21
point /pɔɪnt/ 22
police officer /pəˈliːsˌɒfɪsə, AMˌɔːf-/ 21
policeman /pəˈliːsmən/ 21

policewoman /pəˈliːswumən/ 21
policy /ˈpɒlɪsi/ 6
portrait /ˈpɔːtrət, AMˈpɔːtreɪt/ 14
post /pəʊst/ 1
potato chips /pəˈteɪtəʊˌtʃɪps/ 1
pound /paʊnd/ 21
poverty /ˈpɒvəti/ 6
prescription /prɪˈskrɪpʃən/ 12
presentation /ˌprezənˈteɪʃən, AMˌpriːzen-/ 22
press /pres/ 8
press conference /ˈpresˌkɒnfrəns/ 8
press release /ˈpres rɪˌliːs/ 8
pressure /ˈpreʃə/ 12
pride /praɪd/ 13
private health care /ˌpraɪvɪtˈhelθˌkeə/ 25
private ward /ˌpraɪvɪtˈwɔːd/ 25
profit /ˈprɒfɪt/ 22, 29
promise /ˈprɒmɪs/ 22
promote /prəˈməʊt/ 7
promotion /prəˈməʊʃən/ 7
proposal /prəˈpəʊzəl/ 4
propose /prəˈpəʊz/ 4
provide /prəˈvaɪd/ 18
publicity /pʌˈblɪsɪti/ 8
pull out /ˌpulˈaʊt/ 19
pull over /ˌpulˈəʊvə/ 19
pull something down /ˌpul sʌmθɪŋˈdaʊn/ 11
pull up /ˌpulˈʌp/ 19
pulse /pʌls/ 12
punishment /ˈpʌnɪʃmənt/ 15
put something up /ˌput sʌmθɪŋˈʌp/ 11
puzzled /ˈpʌzəld/ 13

Q

qualify /ˈkwɒlɪfaɪ/ 23
quarrel /ˈkwɒrəl, AMˈkwɔːr-/ 16
quid /kwɪd/ 21

R

race /reɪs/ 28
railroad /ˈreɪlrəʊd/ 1
railway /ˈreɪlweɪ/ 1
rainbow /ˈreɪnbəʊ/ 9
raise /reɪz/ 4
raise a family /ˌreɪz əˈfæmɪli/ 22
rash /ræʃ/ 12
rate /reɪt/ 17
read music /ˌriːdˈmjuːzɪk/ 14

reality /riˈælɪti/ 24
redundant /rɪˈdʌndənt/ 18
refugee /ˌrefjuːˈdʒiː/ 6
release /rɪˈliːs/ 8
relevant /ˈreləvənt/ 7
religious /rɪˈlɪdʒəs/ 5
rescue team /ˈreskjuːˌtiːm/ 10
research /rɪˈsɜːtʃ/ 23
reserve /rɪˈzɜːv/ 9
reside /rɪˈzaɪd/ 21
residence /ˈrezɪdəns/ 21
resident /ˈrezɪdənt/ 11
residential area /ˌrezɪˈdenʃəlˌeəriə/ 3
resort /rɪˈzɔːt/ 3
responsible /rɪˈspɒnsɪbəl/ 26
rhythm /ˈrɪðəm/ 14
ritual /ˈrɪtʃuəl/ 5
room service /ˈruːmˌsɜːvɪsˌˈrum/ 25
roommate /ˈruːmmeɪt, AMˈrummeɪt/ 4
root /ruːt/ 9
rotten /ˈrɒtən/ 27
row /rəʊ/ 19
run /rʌn/ 24
runny nose /ˌrʌniˈnəʊz/ 12
rural /ˈruərəl/ 9
rush /rʌʃ/ 28
rush hour /ˈrʌʃˌaʊə/ 19

S

safe /seɪf/ 25
scan /skæn/ 27
scented /ˈsentɪd/ 27
scheduled /ˈʃedjuːld, AMˈskedʒuːld/ 19
script /skrɪpt/ 2
search dog /ˈsɜːtʃˌdɒg/ 10
second /ˈsekənd/ 22
seed /siːd/ 9
semester /sɪˈmestə/ 1
semi-detached /ˌsemidɪˈtætʃt/ 11
seminar /ˈsemɪnɑː/ 23
sense /sens/ 29
separate /ˈsepəreɪt/ 4
service /ˈsɜːvɪs/ 25
setting /ˈsetɪŋ/ 2
settle /ˈsetəl/ 11
shades /ʃeɪdz/ 21
sharp /ʃɑːp/ 27
shed /ʃed/ 11

shield /ʃiːld/ 10
shiftwork /ˈʃɪftwɜːk/ 18
shocked /ʃɒkt/ 13
shoot down /ˌʃuːtˈdaʊn/ 30
show /ʃəʊ/ 21
sidewalk /ˈsaɪdwɔːk/ 1
sight /saɪt/ 22
signal /ˈsɪgnəl/ 24
sip /sɪp/ 27
sister-in-law /ˈsɪstəɪnˌlɔː/ 4
sit an exam /ˌsɪt ən ɪgˈzæm/ 23
skilled /skɪld/ 18
skills /skɪlz/ 7
skyline /ˈskaɪlaɪn/ 3
slide /slaɪd/ 23
smartphone /ˈsmɑːtˌfəʊn/ 16
sociable /ˈsəʊʃəbəl/ 13
soil /sɔɪl/ 9
soloist /ˈsəʊləʊɪst/ 14
sore throat /ˌsɔːˈθrəʊt/ 12
sound /saʊnd/ 28
soundtrack /ˈsaʊndtræk/ 2
sour /saʊə/ 27
source /sɔːs/ 8
specialize /ˈspeʃəlaɪz/ 23
species /ˈspiːʃiz/ 9
spectator /spekˈteɪtə, AMˈspekteɪtər/ 27
speech /spiːtʃ/ 16
speed of sound /ˌspiːd əvˈsaʊnd/ 28
speed up /ˌspiːdˈʌp/ 28
spirits /ˈspɪrɪts/ 30
stand by /ˌstændˈbaɪ/ 4
standard /ˈstændəd/ 25
stare /steə/ 27
start /stɑːt/ 21
steady income /ˌstediˈɪnkʌm/ 22
stepfather /ˈstepfɑːðə/ 4
stepmother /ˈstepmʌðə/ 4
stick together /ˌstɪk təˈgeðə/ 4
stink /stɪŋk/ 27
stopover /ˈstɒpəʊvə/ 19
store /stɔː/ 3, 24
storey /ˈstɔːri/ 11
street /striːt/ 3
strengths /streŋθs/ 7
stretch /stretʃ/ 28
stride /straɪd/ 28
strike /straɪk/ 18
stroll /strəʊl/ 28
studio flat /ˈstjuːdiəʊˌflæt, AMˈstuː-/ 11
subject /ˈsʌbdʒekt/ 22

126 **Work on your Vocabulary** Upper Intermediate (B2)

Index

submerged /səbˈmɜːdʒd/ 10
subsequently /ˈsʌbsɪkwəntli/ 21
suburbs /ˈsʌbɜːbz/ 3
subway /ˈsʌbweɪ/ 1
sum up /ˌsʌmˈʌp/ 16
sunglasses /ˈsʌŋglɑːsɪz, AM-glæs-/ 21
superstition /ˌsuːpəˈstɪʃən/ 5
supply /səˈplaɪ/ 18
surgeon /ˈsɜːdʒən/ 12
surgery /ˈsɜːdʒəri/ 12, 25
survivor /səˈvaɪvə/ 10
suspicious /səˈspɪʃəs/ 13
sympathetic /ˌsɪmpəˈθetɪk/ 20
sympathy /ˈsɪmpəθi/ 10

T

take a chance /ˌteɪk əˈtʃɑːns/ 22
take advantage of /ˌteɪk ædˈvɑːntɪdʒ ɒv, AM-ˈvæn-, əv/ 25
take after /ˌteɪkˈɑːftə/ 4
take an exam /ˌteɪk ən ɪgˈzæm/ 23
take an unexpected turn /ˌteɪk ənˌʌnɪkˌspektɪdˈtɜːn/ 30
talented /ˈtæləntɪd/ 7
team /tiːm/ 10
television /ˈtelɪvɪʒən, AM-ˈtel·əˌvɪʒ·ən-/ 21
tell the difference /ˌtel ðəˈdɪfrəns/ 22
telly /ˈteli/ 21
term /tɜːm/ 1
terminal /ˈtɜːmɪnəl/ 19
terrace house /ˌterɪsˈhaʊs/ 11
terraced house /ˌterɪstˈhaʊs/ 11
that is to say /ˌðæt ɪs təˈseɪ/ 17
then /ðen/ 21
theology /θiˈɒlədʒi/ 5
thesis /ˈθiːsɪs/ 23
though /ðəʊ/ 17
throat /θrəʊt/ 12
tick /tɪk/ 1
tide /taɪd/ 9
time /taɪm/ 17
to conclude /tə kənˈkluːd/ 17
to make matters worse /təˌmeɪkˌmætəzˈwɜːs/ 29
tolerant /ˈtɒlərənt/ 5
tone /təʊn/ 16
tornado /tɔːˈneɪdəʊ/ 9
tourist trail /ˈtʊərɪstˌtreɪl/ 25

tower block /ˈtaʊəˌblɒk/ 11
town centre /ˌtaʊnˈsentə/ 1
track /træk/ 14
traffic /ˈtræfɪk/ 22
trail /treɪl/ 25
transport /(noun) ˈtrænspɔːt; (verb) trænsˈpɔːt/ 19
trapped /træpt/ 10
trek /trek/ 28
trekking /ˈtrekɪŋ/ 19
trial /traɪəl/ 15
tropical /ˈtrɒpɪkəl/ 9
tube /tjuːb, AM tuːb/ 1
turn up /ˌtɜːnˈʌp/ 19
tutor /ˈtjuːtə, AMˈtuːt-/ 23
tutorial /tjuːˈtɔːriəl, AMˈtuːt-/ 23

U

umbrella /ʌmˈbrelə/ 21
unbearable /ʌnˈbeərəbəl/ 20
underground /ˈʌndəˌgraʊnd/ 1
underline /ˌʌndəˈlaɪn/ 16
unfashionable /ʌnˈfæʃənəbəl/ 20
united /juːˈnaɪtɪd/ 4
upbringing /ˈʌpbrɪŋɪŋ/ 4, 7
update /ʌpˈdeɪt/ 16
upset /ʌpˈset/ 13
used to /ˈjuːst tuː, tə/ 7, 29

V

vacation /vəˈkeɪʃən, AM veɪ-/ 1
verse /vɜːs/ 14
victim /ˈvɪktɪm/ 10
virtual reality /ˌvɜːtʃuəl riˈælɪti/ 24
vocalist /ˈvəʊkəlɪst/ 14
volcano /vɒlˈkeɪnəʊ/ 9

W

ward /wɔːd/ 12, 25
warming /ˈwɔːmɪŋ/ 9
water /ˈwɔːtə/ 30
waterproof /ˈwɔːtəpruːf/ 20
wave /weɪv/ 10
wavy /ˈweɪvi/ 26
weaknesses /ˈwiːknəsɪz/ 7
wealth /welθ/ 6
wealthy /ˈwelθi/ 6
welcoming /ˈwelkəmɪŋ/ 7
welfare /ˈwelfeə/ 6
well-built /ˌwelˈbɪlt/ 26

well-organized /ˌwelˈɔːgənaɪzd/ 20
what is more /ˌwɒt ɪzˈmɔː/ 17
whisper /ˈwɪspə/ 27
widow /ˈwɪdəʊ/ 4
wire /waɪə/ 24
with reference to /ˌwɪðˈrefərəns tuː, AM tə/ 17
with regard to /ˌwɪð rɪˈgɑːd tuː, AM tə/ 17
with respect to /ˌwɪð rɪˈspekt tuː, AM tə/ 17
witness /ˈwɪtnəs/ 15, 27
words /wɜːdz/ 17
workshop /ˈwɜːkʃɒp/ 23
worse /wɜːs/ 29
worthwhile /ˌwɜːθˈwaɪl/ 7
wound /wuːnd/ 12

Y

yell /jel/ 27

Collins
English for Life

Would you like to listen, speak, read and write English fluently?

CEF Level: B1+ Intermediate

Collins English for Life – B1+ Intermediate

Speaking
978-0-00-745783-0
🄲 Includes CD

Writing
978-0-00-746061-8

Reading
978-0-00-745871-4

Listening
978-0-00-745872-1
🄲 Includes CD

- **Authentic:** prepares you for the language you will come across in real life
- **Practical:** learn strategies to understand and to produce natural English
- **Comprehensive:** learn and gain confidence from a broad variety of accents, texts and contexts

Also available in the Collins *Work on your...* series

Communicate like a native English speaker

CEF Level: B1–C2

Collins Work on your Accent
978-0-00-746291-9
🄳 Includes DVD with visual and audio material

Collins Work on your Phrasal Verbs
978-0-00-746466-1

Collins Work on your Idioms
978-0-00-746467-8

If you need help finding our books, please e-mail us at collins.elt@harpercollins.co.uk.

www.collinselt.com

POWERED BY COBUILD